Inside the
Over-the-Counter Market

Inside the Over-the-Counter Market

Tom Wilmot
Chairman and Managing Director, Harvard Securities Group PLC

Woodhead-Faulkner · Cambridge

Published by Woodhead-Faulkner Limited,
Fitzwilliam House, 32 Trumpington Street, Cambridge CB2 1QY

First published 1985
© Tom Wilmot 1985

British Library Cataloguing in Publication Data

Wilmot, Tom
  Inside the over-the-counter market.
  1. Securities—Great Britain—Listing
  I. Title
  332.64'2   HG5432

  ISBN 0-85941-309-8

Research Assistant Mark Pritchard
Designed by Geoff Green
Phototypeset by Wyvern Typesetting Limited, Bristol
Printed in Great Britain by St Edmundsbury Press,
Bury St Edmunds, Suffolk

Contents

Foreword

by Roger Baden-Powell
Chairman of the British Institute of Dealers in Securities (BIDS)

The over-the-counter (OTC) market is a new and dynamic market which has attracted considerable public interest. Those in favour of the growth of a third-tier stock market consider that its development is clearly benefiting a sector of UK industry where new companies can raise equity finance which might otherwise be unavailable to them from The Stock Exchange, its Unlisted Securities Market (USM) or the banks. Those against the OTC market contend that it is nothing but a gamblers' casino, where angels fear to tread. For those in the market and optimistic of its prospects for growth, however, it is generally accepted that there is only one thing worse than being talked about, and that is not being talked about.

I have known Tom Wilmot for a number of years and have watched Harvard Securities grow to its present size despite considerable opposition from the financial establishment. The resulting publicity has ensured that Harvard Securities is better known to the general public than most firms of stockbrokers and it has generated an awareness of the OTC market in the United Kingdom which no affordable advertising campaign could have achieved.

A new 'market' in any commodity begins to develop when a group of dealers gets together in a loose association to offer a service that the public wants. Market makers on the OTC do not often meet in coffee houses as members of Lloyd's and The Stock Exchange used to, since we now have the benefit of telephones and computers. None the less, OTC market makers have suffered the same sort of criticism that stockbrokers used to in the past. In fact, it was a common form of abuse a century or so ago to refer to someone as a 'mere stockjobber', thus depicting a type of person involved in the sort of transactions to which the recognised establishment would not stoop (at least, not while anybody was watching).

In any financial dealings between professionals and members of the public, or, in fact, between members of the public themselves, there is always the danger of a conflict of interest, dishonesty or fraud. Such deals may sometimes be reported in the newspapers, especially if they are large and have some other 'human interest' attraction, but, in general, they are a part of business life which most of us have learned to be wary of, accepting the maxim *caveat emptor*. Once a pattern of dealing begins to develop in a market, however, and once the market begins to assume a distinct identity, any sharp dealings or misrepresentations gain a much higher profile and tend to damage the business of all members of that market by undermining the confidence of the public. We have all seen newspaper headlines to the effect that the 'City is rocked by scandal in Leeds' when, very often, the story has nothing at all to do with the City but the word has been used, because of its encapsulating association with money, as a convenient phrase to stimulate interest in the subsequent article.

Once the identity of a market has been established, therefore, there is a strong necessity to have some form of regulation to safeguard the public interest and also the reputation of those professionals dealing in that market. This can be done either by statute or by means of self-regulation. The United Kingdom is extremely fortunate to have a strong tradition of self-regulation of financial markets. Self-regulation works because it is in the commercial interests of those involved in any trade association to see that it does and because it can be carried out by regulators who understand the problems of the market, since they are in it themselves and can therefore act quickly and effectively to protect the public. The old saying 'If we do not hang together, we will hang separately' tends to bury a lot of commercial rivalry if the sins of one can be visited on another by the publicity surrounding an identifiable market-place. A number of steps are now being taken to regulate the OTC market more effectively and, with this objective in mind, Harvard Securities is playing its part, along with other market makers, to establish a self-regulatory system to match the requirements of the growing market-place.

The OTC market in the United Kingdom is still very young compared to its counterpart in the United States and this book should achieve a greater understanding of the market among members of the public who are bored with building societies and unit trusts and who are prepared to risk a greater involvement in new and growing companies, where both substantial profits and substantial losses can be made.

Author's preface

Although the OTC market in the United Kingdom is a relatively new phenomenon and is still very much in its infancy, it is considered to be the fastest growing equity market in the world. During the last two and a half years it has grown from 26 companies to some 180 and is at the moment capitalised at around £1,000 million, providing great opportunities for new businesses as well as creating new employment. In fact, of the £100 million raised in 1983/84 for BES qualifying companies, Government statistics indicate that in excess of 60% came via direct equity investment in small companies which largely qualified for an OTC quotation. The deregulation of The Stock Exchange and the breakup in 1987/88 of BES funds almost guarantees that the explosive growth of the OTC market will continue unabated. The whole concept of a multi-location, telephone-based market with no central trading floor remains a difficult one with which to contend for the UK investor. However, the growth of the OTC in the United States is a clear indication of the potential interest in the UK market. It is normal with innovative advances of this type for general recognition to be slow, and a crucial element in expanding the market is the education of both professional and private investors in the methods of the OTC. I hope that this book will begin to fill the previous void that existed concerning information on this market. I have tried to cover the market's origins, workings and future as clearly as possible, highlighting the potential of OTC stocks as well as the risks involved when dealing with them. I hope it will prove useful to both professional and private investors and also encourage more and greater involvement in the OTC market, which, after all, is a seed-bed of innovation, wealth and employment.

May 1985 T. G. Wilmot

1 Why has the over-the-counter market developed?

Before dealing with the rationale for the development of the over-the-counter (OTC) market, a brief description of The Stock Market may help professionals and non-professionals alike to understand the vacuum that the OTC market fills.

The Stock Exchange is a fine private club dating back to the 1700s when old coffee houses around London's Royal Exchange were frequented by gentlemen who bought and sold shares in companies on a basis of mutual trust. A share is a part of a company. If a company has a capital of £100, then it is possible to have 100 £1 shares or 200 50 pence shares, etc. If an individual owns 51 £1 shares then he has control of the company. The shares can be bought and sold and ownership of companies can change hands without the acquiescence of the directors if they do not have control of 51% or more. It soon became apparent that to raise capital outside of the personal and business acquaintances of the gentlemen in the coffee houses around the Royal Exchange a formal market-place should be brought into being and in

1773 The Stock Exchange was born. As the name suggests, it is a place where stocks and shares may be exchanged, purchased or encashed.

With a centralised market, stocks and shares could be actively promoted as investments which could be quickly bought and sold, thus leading to a very liquid and vigorous market.

Primarily investors in stocks and shares were the landed rich and industrially wealthy, who were encouraged to protect their wealth by investing in the shares of companies. This investment enabled companies to develop quickly using risk capital, without having to pay interest to banks and money-lenders. The welcome injection of capital into business stimulated and encouraged the dramatic industrial growth seen during the nineteenth century in the United Kingdom.

Private investment

Over the last 50 years, however, the market-place has changed. The emergence of institutional investment has had a far-reaching effect on The Stock Exchange. (Institutional investors, i.e. pension funds, charities, investment trusts, unit trusts, etc., are organisations that put themselves out as managers of investments on behalf of others.) Funds controlled by institutions are immense and growing at an accelerating pace. The institutional dominance of the UK stock market which has developed over the last 30 years can be seen in Table 1.

Table 1 UK holdings of quoted shares

	1957	1963	1969	1975	1981
Individuals	66%	54%	47%	38%	28%
Institutions	18%	24%	32%	43%	57%
Others	17%	21%	21%	19%	15%

Source: The Stock Exchange.

Stockbrokers in the United Kingdom identified institutions as excellent clients; they understand the market and communicate on a professional basis. Processing buying and selling orders is most rewarding to the successful and persistent broker and it is no wonder that a large number of them moved away from their private client business and invested in corporate research, using specialist salesmen to deal with the large institutions.

This move left the private client in a vacuum, however – he was used to dealing in shares on a personal basis, but, as the emphasis shifted to the institutional client, nobody seemed really interested in his business unless he had £25,000 to £1 million to place in a discretionary managed account. (A discretionary account is where a client gives control of his money to a third party who is entitled to buy and sell on behalf of the client without referring to him before or after trading, although the third party will usually provide dealing statements at the end of every six months. Non-discretionary, on the other hand, means that a client has to give his written or verbal consent before a transaction can be completed on his behalf.) The only alternative left to the private investor was to invest with the unit trusts or investment trusts, etc. – and these were, ironically, the very institutions whose entry into the market-place had forced large numbers of private clients into the financial wilderness.

This has resulted in a marked fall over the last 30 years in the proportion of equities held by private individuals, as can be seen from Table 1. Today, only around 2 million people in the United Kingdom, or 5% of the adult population, directly own shares. This compares with 42 million, or 25% of the adult population, in the United States. The fact that this increased institutional investment is normally in blue-chip companies also means that little is being done to foster growth in the small-to-medium-sized company sector.

Stock Exchange listing

The past two decades have also witnessed a significant and continuing reduction in the extent to which UK companies have been coming to the securities markets in search of equity finance. Certainly, the fiscal bias in favour of loan finance has to a certain extent discouraged companies from utilising equity as a source of long-term finance, but the escalating fees for companies seeking a quotation have been another major factor.

In the late 1960s and early 1970s an average of some 50 companies per annum achieved listed status, but between 1974 and 1979 new admissions were running at less than half this rate. Although there has been a slight reversal of this trend as the memories of 1974 recede (when falling share prices and general disillusionment with the stock markets made the idea of a market flotation virtually unthinkable), the costs associated with a full listing are still prohibitive for many companies.

There are other reasons, too, for the steady decline in applications for admission to The Stock Exchange. First, the general economic climate has been unhelpful to small and medium-sized companies, especially if an owner sought to dispose of part of his company as a way of capitalising on previous effort. Low real profitability has the effect of greatly reducing the extent to which businesses can expect to finance themselves from internally generated funds and means that prices for securities are kept at a low level, thus discouraging any offer for sale of shares. In the mean time rates of inflation have greatly increased the working capital requirement of many companies even though the real volume of output may have remained unchanged, with the result that profits are used to finance the day-to-day running of a company instead of being reinvested.

Second, it has been frequently suggested that the conditions imposed by The Stock Exchange for access to the listed market represent a real disincentive to listing. For an initial sale of securities by way of a full quote, The Stock Exchange expects a company to be able to show at least a five-year trading record and has certain requirements as to the contents of a company's prospectus as well as onerous disclosure requirements. Indeed, although the Stock Exchange minimum size for a listing is a market capitalisation of £0.7 million, in practice the minimum size before an issue of shares becomes economic is around £5 million (equivalent to pre-tax profits of approximately £1 million). The consequent professional fees and advertising costs add to the expense of a flotation, which, including commissions, may easily amount to between 5% and 10% of the proceeds. Of the costs incurred there is a very high element of fixed costs, resulting in the net amount raised being wholly unrelated to the size of the issue. This problem has been particularly acute for companies raising only relatively small amounts of capital where in fact the issue costs have become totally disproportionate. It is a fact that this rapid increase in costs has deterred companies from coming to the listed market. Obviously, inflation accounts for some of the increase, but the large upgrading in disclosure requirements and the consequent increase in accountancy and legal fees have caused the bulk of the escalation. What is more, potential investors have come to expect weighty and informative prospectuses. On top of this a prospectus is quite rightly seen as a marketing document as a whole, being a complete reflection of the company's activities. As such, there are considerable PR, presentation and printing costs.

The reduction, in September 1977, by The Stock Exchange of the required, minimum amount of a new company's equity which has to be made available to the investing public, from 35% to 25%, was met with mixed feelings. Certainly, from the point of view of the aspiring company, a reduction in the amount of equity which has to be released on to the market was very welcome. However, this limited marketability was not at all well received by the long-term investing institutions. The influence of the major institutions on the market-place could well be a significant factor in the decline in applications for full listing. Undoubtedly, institutional funds dominate the equity markets and due to their obligations (e.g. payment of insurance claims or pensions) they are inherently risk averse. Therefore, pressure may well have been placed upon the Quotations Department of The Stock Exchange to retain the strict requirements of companies seeking a listing. Thus, small, high-risk companies have essentially been squeezed out of the equity market-place.

The Unlisted Securities Market (USM)

The Wilson Committee Review of the functioning of financial institutions in 1980 recognised the need 'to improve the market mechanisms for dealing in unlisted securities ... in order to improve the marketability of equity stakes in small companies'. At this time, dealing in unlisted securities by members of The Stock Exchange was only allowed under Rule 163 of the Stock Exchange Rule Book, which was later revised and reclassified as Rule 535. Rule 163(2) allowed trading in small, unquoted UK companies and was originally intended to enable relatively infrequent transactions to take place in the shares of small, public companies. Rule 163(3) applied specifically to mineral exploration companies. Each company was, and still is, briefly scrutinised by The Stock Exchange and each deal in the shares required specific Stock Exchange approval. Although the jobber takes a turn (the profit resulting from the difference between the buying price and the selling price of a share) and the broker charges commission, each trade in Rule 163(2) shares is effectively a matched bargain with the jobber putting through the transaction for a small turn. The Stock Exchange will refuse permission to deal in shares where it considers that the Rule 163 facility is being abused. For example, Intervision was delisted in March 1982 by The Stock Exchange Council as it was being traded far too often under this rule.

Following publicity gained as a result of the Wilson Committee in 1978 the number of deals under Rule 163(2) grew rapidly, with a number of companies issuing securities specifically with a view to trading under this rule. This, combined with the recommendations made in the interim report of the Wilson Committee, prompted The Stock Exchange to issue a discussion document in December 1979 on the development of a market in unlisted securities. The general response to the idea was good, the proposals being praised for their innovative approach in encouraging new issues. After a number of amendments this document actually formed the basis for the Unlisted Securities Market, which was launched on 10 November 1980. For the first time in its history The Stock Exchange offered a three-tier market in company securities – the first tier being a full listing, the second tier being the USM and the third tier consisting of dealings still made possible by the new Rule 535(2).

One of the early driving forces behind the USM was Licensed Dealers Tringhall. Dennis Poll of Tringhall identified a market need and set about floating companies on the USM. However, his method of ensuring that Tringhall's issues were successful ultimately engineered its downfall. Any shareholder in Tringhall shares was given priority of allotment of any new USM issue floated by Tringhall. With its earlier issues being very successful it did not matter that most of the investors at the issue price were speculators purely and simply interested in short-term gain (i.e. stags); the novelty of the USM ensured a reasonable after-market which allowed them to take their profit. However, as the USM became recognised and more and more issues were floated, Tringhall found that its issues had little or no after-market. This resulted in discounts on the issue price after the shares were floated. Investors and stags alike became disillusioned. Tringhall in its heyday had taken sizeable stakes in issues which became virtually unsaleable.

The demise of Tringhall has been well tabulated, but it is probable that without its early enthusiasm the USM would have taken a further two to three years to reach its current level of success. In fact, the USM now includes well over 350 companies with a stream of others waiting to get on. With less stringent requirements than the main Stock Exchange and much reduced costs, the USM has great attractions for young, growing companies. It is interesting to note that in the initial drafting document the USM was meant as a transitional market, with companies eventually graduating to the Official List. This has not proved to be the case, however, with most companies preferring to remain on the unlisted market, and this may well have implications for the OTC market, which has already been branded as a 'nursery slope'.

The USM has filled a clear need. In the five years prior to the establishment of the market only 60 companies went public in the United Kingdom, an average of 12 a year. Since 1980, an average of 60 companies each year have gone public on the USM, and during 1984 there were, in fact, some 100 flotations.

The Business Start-up Scheme (BSS)

Initially, the introduction of the USM took some of the impetus away from moves towards a full OTC market. However, it soon became clear that the USM had not gone quite far enough. The requirement of a three-year trading record (even though this can be waived in exceptional circumstances) meant that start-up companies were denied access to equity finance; at least 10% of the equity had to be sold and the General Undertaking signed by all USM entrants placed onerous disclosure requirements on young, growing companies.

In the 1981 Budget the Government introduced the Business Start-up Scheme. This scheme offered tax incentives to investors prepared to risk their capital in small and young companies. It was hoped that this scheme would provide the venture capital so desperately needed to fund tomorrow's businesses today. Unfortunately, the BSS was received with cautious pessimism and during its two-year life only around £20 million was raised.

In the 1983 Budget the scheme was improved, extended and renamed the Business Expansion Scheme (see Chapter 6). This scheme allowed major tax concessions to private investors prepared to invest capital directly into small companies. Curiously enough, the Government developed the idea a step further and stipulated that companies funded via the BES would lose BES status if they were listed in any formal way. This precluded a full Stock Exchange listing and it even precluded USM listing. It did not, however, preclude BES companies from a listing on the emerging OTC market.

Emergence of the OTC market

The Stock Exchange view clearly was that the so-called third-tier equity market under Rule 535(2) was only a temporary measure and that the introduction of USM would see an end to dealings under this rule. However, as in the intervening years the USM itself has become 'institutionalised' and now looks at more substantial companies, the third-tier segment of the equity financing structure has come to the fore again. It has long been recognised in the United Kingdom that small businesses have special difficulties in obtaining finance. As far back as 1931 the MacMillan

Committee identified a gap in the availability of finance for small and medium-sized companies which were too small to justify a full flotation. The Bolton Committee Inquiry on small firms in 1971 again highlighted that small firms are at a considerable disadvantage in financial markets, due to loans being more expensive and security requirements generally more stringent. External equity is more difficult to find and, even then, may be obtainable only on relatively unfavourable terms. There can be little doubt that the equity gap identified just over half a century ago still exists and that this deficiency may well be placing a constraint on the growth and expansion of small businesses. It is fast-growing firms which are most likely to experience a lack of capital. This shortage of funds has two main consequences, which in turn could adversely affect the national economy and hamper any attempts to rebuild a more competitive UK industrial base. First, a lack of capital will reduce the number of business 'start-ups' (new companies are considered by many to be the most effective answer to the problem of unemployment). Second, any shortage of development capital will undoubtedly place constraints on the expansion of established businesses. Banks have often been singled out for not investing in UK industry or for preferring established companies – however dubious their prospects – to the small, adventurous companies of the future. Indeed, Lord Lever, a former Cabinet Minister, made a forceful case criticising the clearing banks in an article in *The Times*: 'Many of Britain's economic ills can be traced in whole or in part to the historic distortion of our credit system; the financial arrangements which enabled us to buy our homes are not available to our factories.' He maintained that one of the great British failings was an inability to channel savings into investment and he gave this grave warning: 'Unless we act to revive investment, our decline is assured at a more rapid rate than in the last decade.'

According to national income figures, bank borrowing currently represents around 52% of the external financing requirements of industrial and commercial companies, whereas ordinary share issues represent only 2%. The problem cannot therefore be laid exclusively at the feet of the clearing banks; there are obviously serious deficiencies in the UK securities markets.

It is of great importance to small businesses that an adequate proportion of their long-term finance takes the form of equity, which does not carry the inflexible servicing obligations of loan capital. Since the USM is increasingly looking for companies with a substantial trading record, small companies seeking an injection of equity are faced with very unfavourable propositions through private placings. Both stockbrokers and venture capital companies will offer deals to companies too immature to reach the USM. However, the limited number of potential investors, the relative illiquidity of the shares and the degree of risk attached to any single investment in a small, high-risk business are all reflected in the terms offered. This usually means that expansion is inhibited or else financed by loans, which is clearly unacceptable for fast-growing businesses coming up against gearing constraints. The introduction of the USM in 1980 has gone some way towards filling the equity gap first highlighted by MacMillan. However, a proper market segment for small company shares clearly needs to be developed. Although dealings in such companies were permitted under Rule 163(2) (now Rule 535(2)), generally there has been no mechanism for this type of company to procure the initial finance. Furthermore, the average investor has never heard of this facility and if he wishes to take a stake in a seemingly high-risk company he is forced either to participate in a private placing or, alternatively, to look to the foreign markets.

With the groundswell of opinion that neither The Stock Exchange nor the USM are fulfilling the requirements of smaller and new businesses and with the increased dominance of institutional, rather than private, investment in listed companies, the recent emergence of the OTC market offers greater potential for industry and investors alike, providing a much-needed third-tier segment of the UK equities market.

Early days

In fact, the first version of an OTC market was effectively born in the United Kingdom as early as 1972. This was M. J. H. Nightingale & Co. (now known as Granville & Co.). As a licensed dealer in securities, its objective was to offer an alternative to The Stock Market, both for companies that wished to raise finance and for investors.

M. J. H. Nightingale & Co. aimed at large unlisted companies which required their shares to be placed among investors but which felt that a full listing involved too much publicity and was an expensive method of raising equity, since at that time the minimum equity allowance set by The Stock Exchange required at least 35% of the total equity to be on offer. These companies wished to see their shares in firm hands so that they were not vulnerable to an unwanted take-over bid or, indeed, to outside influences which could result from any one individual or group of individuals or companies acquiring a significant amount of the shares floated. Essentially they wished to stay firmly private, but, due to circumstances beyond their immediate control, funds had to be raised via the placing of existing shares or new shares. The death of a major shareholder or the requirement for hard cash by the second or third generation were strong reasons for finding a market where funds could be raised discretely.

M. J. H. Nightingale & Co.'s service provided an institutionally based market with around 80–90 of Britain's leading financial institutions accounting for some 70–75%

of the trading volume by value, the remaining 25–30% being held by private investors. The shares would initially be placed with a number of major institutions and traded thereafter on a matched market, with buyer and seller being matched by market maker at identical share prices and a 1.25% commission (calculated on the consideration) being charged to both buyer and seller.

M. J. H. Nightingale & Co. can therefore guarantee the independence of the companies in which it makes a market because dealing on a matched-bargain basis it is always fully in the picture as to who is trying to buy and who is trying to sell. Unwanted share purchasers will find themselves unable to acquire a significant stake in companies now quoted by Granville & Co. Indeed, of the 28 companies to join the M. J. H. Nightingale/Granville market, 26 are still on their own OTC market. Only Henry Sykes PLC (to a full Stock Exchange listing) and Twinlock PLC (to the USM) have left, and both succumbed to take-over bids within two years of leaving. These statistics in themselves underline the success that M. J. H. Nightingale & Co. has had in providing its version of the OTC market.

Later developments

The next company to develop OTC trading was Harvard Securities Limited, incorporated in 1973 by M. J. Glickman, a Canadian resident, who saw an opening in the United Kingdom for an OTC market in speculative share issues. From the very outset Harvard Securities created and promoted a market which was in all respects very different from the Granville & Co. OTC market. Harvard Securities positioned itself firmly as a dual-capacity dealer outside of The London Stock Exchange, making a market in speculative share issues. As a market maker, Harvard Securities would normally always quote a two-way share price and be prepared to take back stock on to its own book. This was, in the early 1970s, a very bold and radical move, and one which attracted a great deal of criticism from the financial establishment. Indeed, the legacy of related bad publicity still lingers on in some circles, although this is gradually diminishing as Harvard Securities is accepted as part of the financial community. The main thrust of Harvard Securities' business (unlike Granville & Co.) is the private client. This investment service is strictly on a very American, no-frills basis. Harvard Securities found that it could provide a good private client service in more speculative issues and still make a profit. By 1984 it had some 45,000 non-discretionary private clients, clearly demonstrating the need for private client 'broker-dealers' in the United Kingdom. In its early days Harvard Securities made a market in a number of American OTC stocks, which were marketed to private investors in the United Kingdom. These were usually lines of 'Founder' stock, subject to SEC Rule 144 and, as such, having restricted selling rights in the United States.

Following this, the OTC market stayed quiet for a while, apart from a small offering by Harvard Securities in July 1977. This was Tarag Growth Holdings, a Jersey-based company specialising in investing in commodities and offering UK investors the opportunity to become involved in commodities on a limited-risk basis. Harvard Securities raised £250,000 and traded the shares on a jobbing market-making basis, taking risk as a principal and providing a liquid market to would-be buyers and sellers.

Owing to its highly controversial and innovative move in creating an alternative share market, Harvard Securities rapidly gained a very high public profile. A consequence of the disproportionate amount of publicity that grew up around the company, however, was that numerous finance proposals were made from young, energetic companies. This is something which still occurs and it has provided an opportunity for Harvard Securities to become an important Issuing House, playing a crucial role in raising equity finance for small companies. Indeed, since early 1983 Harvard Securities has been bringing companies to the OTC market with frightening regularity.

At the time of writing, Harvard Securities has been involved in 25 major public flotations, together with several rights issues, raising over £30 million for UK industry. Harvard Securities has always been at the forefront in the establishment of an active OTC share market in the United Kingdom.

Despite being heavily criticised for its speculative nature, the OTC does have a very valid role to play. As already established, the public issue of equity instruments of small companies at an early stage in their development is a desirable component of any equity financing system, hence, there should be a segment catering exclusively for companies that are young, small and highly risky. Having a clearly-segmented market will contribute to the perception and understanding by the public of the different risks associated with each segment. For companies, the differences between segments are emphasised by having different entry requirements for each level.

Such a market is without doubt a very desirable element of any equity financing system, offering to a suitable firm a useful facility either for raising fresh development funds as part of basic corporate strategy or as a method of capitalising on previous effort. The existence of a capital market to which small companies can realistically aspire should make it easier for them to obtain start-up finance. The market will also provide the essential element of flexibility lacking in other methods of raising equity finance (e.g. a private placing). Moreover, the prices established in this market facilitate the fair valuation of equity instruments which are to be used in private placements, and its existence assures participants in private financings that a market for the shares in which they have invested can be established. This is a point particularly relevant to BES investment and illustrates how the existence of the OTC can even benefit companies yet to go public.

The benefit to the UK economy of channelling money into new growth companies is obvious. It may help offset the erosion, over a long period of competitiveness, of traditional areas of industry, since small, growing companies are the ones most likely to provide significant employment in the future and replace the declining industrial sectors of the economy. There is generally no lack of innovative ideas and the OTC capital markets could play a major role in converting these ideas into profitable companies.

As the OTC is seemingly now established in its market niche, it is important that, in the midst of the changes currently taking place in the City of London and generally in the area of financial services, this third tier is not swept away. The lowest segment is arguably the most important, as it is the point of entry for small, young companies and may be the first step on the ladder towards a full listing on The Stock Exchange. As such, entry to this particular segment must not be impeded by minimum requirements as to age, size or intrinsic risk, nor by high entry costs or continuing fees.

2 The OTC market – a guide for investors

OTC trading

The OTC market in the United Kingdom is essentially the trading in stocks and shares outside of the controls and requirements of The Stock Exchange. Transactions are carried out by a variety of licensed dealers in securities, which frequently buy and sell for their own account and which usually specialise in certain issues. Investors may buy or sell directly from the dealer willing to buy or sell stock or shares.

There are currently 15 market makers on the OTC, quoting prices in the shares of companies which do not, in most cases, meet the listing requirements of the London Stock Exchange. A market maker is a licensed dealer in securities which is entitled to act in a dual capacity, i.e. as a principal (like a stockjobber) and as an agent (like a stockbroker). This enables a market maker to make a market in the shares of individual companies and at the same time act on behalf of private clients who may wish to buy or sell shares in those companies.

Each of the market makers is, effectively, a mini stock market, offering companies and dealing clients the same sort of facilities offered by The Stock Exchange, but on a much smaller scale. The majority of OTC-quoted companies are new or emerging businesses with, in most cases, less than three years' audited accounts. They could also be 'shell-type' companies which have in the long-distant past enjoyed a Stock Exchange listing but for one reason or another have been de-listed only to be revived by entrepreneurial initiative and the OTC market.

Although there is often an outrageous level of risk associated with OTC stocks, this is compensated for by the market's outstanding growth potential; in the OTC market today are the giants of tomorrow. Polaroid, Apple Computers, Tampax, MCI, Communications Intel Corporation, Beckshire Hathaway Inc. and Tandem Computers are all examples of ideas which have grown and matured on the OTC market in the United States. In the early days, US companies regarded the OTC as the nursery slopes prior to a full, mainboard listing. But even larger companies are now staying on the OTC as the increasing number of market makers allows a high level of liquidity. MCI, for instance, traded 360,330,000 shares during 1984 through its 28 market makers at an average share price of around $7. Similarly, the Intel Corporation, with some 113,505,000 shares outstanding, is capitalised at $3,778,140,000, or nearly three and a half times the total market capitalisation of the OTC in the United Kingdom! Even Southland Financial Corporation, which in 1984 was number 50 in the NASDAQ (National Association of Securities Dealers Automated Quotations) list of market leaders, was capitalised at some $521,906,000 – not far short of the capitalisation of the whole UK market.

Most of the 15 market makers are currently private companies with few outside shareholders. These licensed dealers in securities are enjoying the benefits of a new market offering tremendous opportunity without competition from external predators, such as overseas stockbrokers, merchant banks, etc. – but this freedom of movement and lack of competition will not last for long. There have already been a number of rumours concerning major institutions looking to acquire licensed dealers. Of the licensed dealers, Harvard Securities is by far the largest, Granville & Co. is probably second, Hill Woolgar third, Afcor fourth, Ravendale fifth, N. K. Cosgrave & Co. sixth, Prior Harwin seventh and the rest of the pack rather bunched up and some distance from the leaders.

Licensed dealers in securities are companies which hold a principal's licence granted either by the Department of Trade or by an association of dealers in securities recognised by the Secretary for Trade and Industry under s. 15 of the Prevention of Fraud (Investments) Act 1958. Each licensed dealer employs staff who are required to hold a representative's licence before they can effect transactions on behalf of private clients or institutions; these licences are also obtained from the Department of Trade or a recognised association. There are currently some 530 holders of principal's licences and 1,400 holders of representative's licences. Only around 30 to 40 holders of principal's licences use them as a main part of their day-to-day business, but, as the OTC market develops, this number will increase dramatically.

Active licensed dealers who use their licence as the mainstay of their business operate in a similar fashion to stockbrokers. If a client gives a purchase or sale order, the licensed representative writes a booking slip. The booking slip is passed down to the computer room so that the relative contract can be prepared and sent to the client. To complete the balance of the paperwork resulting from that purchase or sale transaction, the licensed dealer will have general office staff. They will try to ensure that the extensive paperwork resulting from any one bargain is completed without a hitch. There will be departments or individuals looking after registration, rights, dividends, sold transfers, bought transfers, client ledgers, brokers' ledgers, stock positions, principal accounts, clients' accounts, etc., and the usual office manager and company secretary.

Most licensed dealers separate account executives (dealers) from their market makers. There are several ways in which shares are currently quoted on an OTC basis.

1 *Jobbing market.* The licensed dealer takes a principal risk and is prepared to deal at the price and size quoted whether or not this suits its book position. When dealing as a jobbing market maker it will (like a jobber) have a book position that is either long (e.g. 10,000 shares on its book position) or short (e.g. minus 10,000 shares). In the case of a short position the market maker is under pressure to cover the short to ensure that it can deliver the shares to the buying client (the share price would eventually have to rise to attract sellers to the book). However, in every share in which the licensed dealer is jobbing, potential dealing clients will not be told its book position, so it is up to the individual clients to decide whether or not the price offered is acceptable. The jobbing market maker will seek to make a principal profit out of its book positions.

2 *Matched markets or matched bargains.* The market maker in this instance does not take a position; it simply matches willing buyer and willing seller and usually charges a commission to both parties.

3 *Basis or negotiable price.* Here again the market maker does not take a position. It will listen to and negotiate with potential buyers and sellers to try to establish a price at which a transaction can be completed. This may take weeks, months or even years. A basis price is only a guide to the value of a share and actual trading prices may vary by a large margin.

Individuals inside market-making companies (also known as market makers) take the decisions as to the minute by minute variations in the price and size their company is prepared to trade in on a particular share. If, for instance, someone wishes to trade in Thew Engineering PLC 1 pence ordinary shares, he will simply telephone his licensed dealer and ask for market makers. When he gets through to an individual market maker he will ask for the price and size in Thew ordinary. He (i.e. the market maker) will then quote the size and price. As he is acting as a principal on behalf of the licensed dealer, the trade can be completed there and then. If, for example, the market maker quotes 35–38 pence in 10,000 shares, this means that 10,000 shares may be sold at 35 pence or that 10,000 shares may be bought at 38 pence. The difference between the two prices is known as the spread and is effectively the dealer's profit margin, as there is no commission charged. If someone wishes to trade in a larger amount he simply asks for a price in a larger size. If he has a large amount to sell it is usually better to keep this information to himself. The dealer may quote 1 pence out in 25,000 and this means that it (the dealer) will buy 25,000 shares at 34 pence or sell at 39 pence. If this size is still not large enough, the price in a larger amount may be quoted. The dealing terminology and method of dealing are very similar to those used by stockbrokers but when dealing with a licensed dealer one is also effectively dealing direct with the jobber whose function is to make a profit out of every transaction. It is possible to try to negotiate with the market maker for a better price and selling or buying limits may be left with him.

As the OTC market develops, it will become progressively common for shares quoted OTC to be traded by more than one licensed dealer. So, when wishing to buy or sell, check around; the increased competition between market makers will effectively narrow the spread and often it will be possible to deal at a choice price (i.e. the same for buying and selling). Since a licensed dealer does not charge commission when acting as a principal, any purchase or sale will only attract a 1% Government transfer stamp levy on the consideration. Dealing with a licensed dealer can therefore be comparatively cheap. Dealing through a member of the British Institute of Dealers in Securities (BIDS) (see page 65) will bring a further charge of 30 pence per transaction on bargains up to £1,500 and 65 pence per transaction on bargains over £1,500. The money raised by this levy is being used by BIDS to form a compensation fund via an insurance scheme, which will help investors who lose money as a result of the failure of a BIDS member to meet its commitments.

Several OTC market makers match bargains. The most well known is Granville & Co. (see page 12). The OTC market operated by Granville & Co. is claimed to be élitist in concept and seeks to attract good-quality industrial and commercial companies that are leaders in a particular industry or industrial sector or in a specific geographical area. Its trading method is for buyer and seller to be matched by the market maker at an identical price, with a 1.25% commission being charged to both parties. Granville & Co. argues that this is the most satisfactory way for it to complete business, as it has designed its company to meet the requirements of industrialists and long-term investors rather than to provide a means by which short-term investors can transact bargains with the objective of making speculative gains. Granville & Co. states that the most distinguishing features of its OTC market are that it extensively monitors transactions in the shares of the companies it quotes to ensure that the independence of the companies is preserved, and that its companies tend to have relatively few, fairly sophisticated investors.

Other market makers match bargains and, indeed, this is the basis for dealing under the Stock Exchange Rule 535(2) (see page 6). However, matched bargain trading can cause problems, inasmuch as the share price quoted is tested only when a willing buyer and a willing seller get together. A share price can therefore stay at a high level for a long period only to plummet when a buyer is found at a substantially lower level. Obviously, the opposite can also happen but usually it's trying to sell a share that tests the price quoted. CDFC (Commercial Development and Finance Corporation – the reconstructed Tringhall) was priced at around the 30 pence level in February 1983; the price had remained at this level for some two months. There was a list of some 260 separate selling orders but, because there were no buyers, a trade could not be matched and the price stayed at around the 25 pence level. When a buyer appeared a trade could be matched and the shares fell immediately from between 20 and 25 pence to between $7\frac{1}{2}$ and 11 pence. A week later the share price had fallen again to between 4 and 7 pence.

The danger inherent in matching bargains can be seen if one considers that if an investor or a corporation has a large principal position in shares which are traded on this basis, for very little cost the shares can be moved higher, thus 'increasing' the apparent total value of the holding. Simply placing a buy order at a higher level and arranging for a 'friend' to place a simultaneous selling order at the same level means that – hey presto – the price goes up. The capitalisation of the company is increased and everything looks rosy until sellers appear. Even the arrival of a seller is not a problem until a buyer turns up at a similar price. Abuses of this nature can so easily happen in a market which is not regularly tested and it is important that all matched bargain makers clearly state on their contract notes or in their terms of trade that the price of the shares purchased is calculated on a matched bargain basis and that no guarantee can be given that any sale order can be effected. Private clients, in particular, are vulnerable and may not readily understand why they have to wait an unspecified period for a buyer to appear.

BIDS clearly requires its members to state if they are simply matching bargains. Under its rules and regulations, a jobbing market maker is required to complete a trade with a minimum £250 worth of business on the prices it quotes. This may not sound a large amount, but it effectively allows the price quoted to be continually tested. If someone wishes to sell 5,000 shares but the market maker quotes 45–48 pence in 1,000 shares then he should simply sell 1,000 shares and continue ringing up until he has retailed the whole amount. He may not like the average sale price but at least he has sold his position. Unlike the matched market maker the jobbing market maker cannot artificially hold the share price up against market forces, except at considerable cost and risk. The likelihood of artificial prices diminishes as the number of jobbing market makers in any one share increases.

Basis or negotiable price markets are just an indication of a price at which negotiations for purchase or sale should begin. There are no set rules and any purchase of shares which are quoted on a negotiable price basis leaves the buyer in an unenviable position.

'Bid only' or 'offered only' discloses the way in which the market maker is prepared to trade. If the price is 'bid only' then a trader can only sell to the market maker. A purchase could be made, but very much on a negotiation basis and it would probably be completed at a price which bears little resemblance to the 'bid' price quoted. 'Offered only' is the reverse of 'bid only'. A trader may purchase at the price quoted but any sale is subject to negotiation.

A primary market maker is the main market maker in a particular share or stock, otherwise known as the 'shop', and is usually the licensed dealer which originally introduced the stock or share to the OTC market. As the primary market maker is closely involved with the company, its share and the marketing, it is most likely to offer the most liquid of markets in that particular share. Secondary market makers may be able to compete price-wise but when it comes to selling or buying a line of shares it is best to try the primary market maker first. For instance, Hard Rock Cafe ordinary shares are currently quoted by three market makers. But if Harvard Securities quotes the shares at, say, 66–70 pence in 10,000 shares, Afcor quotes 67–71 pence in 5,000 and Prior Harwin quotes 68–72 pence in 2,500 shares, for a buyer, Harvard Securities is obviously the best proposition. However, on small sales it would be better to trade with Afcor or Prior Harwin. If someone wanted to trade outside of the sizes quoted, he would probably find that the primary market maker produces the most commercial deal in size. The primary market maker knows where to go for stock as it will have placed most of the shares in the first place and, being close to and actively interested in the company, it has a vested interest in seeing that any line of stock overhanging the market is placed as soon as possible. A list of OTC market makers in the United Kingdom can be seen in Appendix I.

Investing in OTC shares

It is important to note at the outset that all the private clients of market making licensed dealers (members of BIDS) are non-discretionary; it is the client who makes the buy/sell decision and there are no managed portfolios. That is the way it is at the moment and that is the way it must always be, so that the position of the licensed dealer, with the dual jobbing/broking capacity, is not compromised. Furthermore, all clients must give their permission to be approached by a licensed dealer and 'cold' calls are not permitted. These conditions are strictly adhered to and contained in statutory form in the Licensed Dealers (Conduct of Business) Rules 1983.

The OTC in the United Kingdom is at present a fragmented, telephone-based market. Although all deals are executed over the telephone (as in the OTC in the United States), investors will find it just as simple as dealing with a conventional stockbroker. A client wishing to deal in any particular stock must first find out which licensed dealers actually make a market in that stock and then call them to obtain a price; once a satisfactory bargain has been struck between client and dealer, the transaction is detailed in a contract note and dispatched in the same day's post. Most of the licensed dealers operate a stock market, fortnightly account system and unless the shares are newly issued (and therefore not registered) there will be the normal 1% stamp duty charge. A number of OTC shares can be dealt with under Rule 535(2) (see page 6), which permits occasional dealings in unquoted shares through The Stock Exchange, and an investor should perhaps bear this in mind if he is at all worried about the liquidity of OTC shares.

Risk

A widely held opinion, traditionalist in its origins, is that high-risk, speculative investments should not be made available to the public. However, this is a view which is hopelessly outdated. Institutional and individual investors, and their advisers, in today's securities markets are well aware of the risk/return characteristics of available investments. The portfolio strategy of diversification is now widely followed by investors and, although the risk of a particular small company may appear unacceptably high on its own, the shares may be attractive as a small part of a portfolio. Furthermore, the average investor in the United Kingdom has access to a whole range of foreign 'high-risk' stocks and efforts to restrict the flow of domestic stocks of this nature appear futile.

It should also be remembered that the risk associated

with small-company shares is not artificially created. The degree of risk reflects the innovativeness of the company and the fact that it will usually be at a very early stage in its history and therefore subject to a great number of external influences. Clearly, the OTC is at the more speculative end of the equity markets and, as such, dealings in OTC stocks are of a high-risk nature. It is not the market-place in which to risk one's life savings or money which is crucial to one's personal solvency. It is often said of the OTC in the United States that out of any ten stocks brought to the market, three or four will be real high-flyers, two will fall along the wayside and the remainder will perform adequately. This also seems applicable to the developing OTC in the United Kingdom and already some spectacular capital gains have been achieved. Certainly, the small private investor can do very well on the market. With good timing and a little luck, healthy gains are possible and investment itself can become an interesting hobby, which is not only exciting for the investor, but should also be of economic importance to the country.

In order to reduce risk, it is almost essential that an investor diversifies his personal portfolio, so that his investments cover the widest possible spread of opportunities. This may, therefore, include at one end gilt-edged securities (i.e. government bonds) and, at the other, stock quoted on the OTC. Obviously, the relative proportions invested in the different types of stock will depend on the individual's risk preference and the amount invested will reflect his personal circumstances. The portfolio strategy is a simple yet effective way of reducing overall risk exposure in equity trading and is widely practised by individuals and institutions alike. Portfolio selection and monitoring is obviously up to the individual, but surely we are nearing the day when an OTC unit trust will be available? Such a unit trust could commit funds to a wide range of leading OTC stocks, which could then be professionally managed by an independent body. Thus, prospective investors could be provided with professional portfolio management in a market which should provide quite spectacular returns.

However, it is fair to say that it is advisable for only a small percentage of any investment portfolio to be committed to OTC stocks, although it should be borne in mind that, as OTC stocks are primarily capital growth orientated, they should be attractive to high-rate income tax payers. Clearly, such investments become even more attractive when they are eligible for tax relief under the Business Expansion Scheme (see Chapter 6). The existence of this Government-promoted scheme will undoubtedly help to reduce the overall cost of an investment and therefore reduce the amount of capital exposed to risk.

Following OTC shares

One major problem in the early stages of the UK market was the scarcity of reliable information on companies traded OTC and, in addition, firm price quotes were difficult to obtain.

The first major move to provide some standardised price information was by Prior Harwin, which circulated a weekly 'pink sheet'. Drawing on the US tradition, this was simply a sheet of prices distributed around other dealers and to a client list. This included stocks traded by a number of dealers but many of the prices were quoted as 'basis' only (i.e. as little more than a starting point for negotiations) and, in any case, these quotations were very quickly out of date. Therefore, the only reliable method of obtaining firm prices on individual stocks was to actually telephone the dealer concerned and ask him. This was obviously a cumbersome and time-consuming task and as the market grew, with more and more investors involved, a need was created for more exposure. Primarily, this need has been met by advertising in daily newspapers, which all the major licensed dealers now do. Harvard Securities, for example, publishes an OTC price guide in *Financial Weekly*, *The Standard* (the London evening paper), the *Daily Telegraph* (every Thursday) and, under the auspices of BIDS, a combined advert is placed in the *Sunday Telegraph*. There are also a number of specialist magazines, such as the *OTC Magazine*, the *USM/OTC Review* and *Personal Investor*.

A further innovation by Harvard Securities is the screening of prices on the Prestel electronic information system. The full range of shares quoted by Harvard is available on the Prestel system and the prices quoted are updated daily. The relatively high cost of using Prestel has meant that there are only a fairly limited number of individual users as yet, but this number is growing and the cost of using the system may well fall as a result. The importance of having prices quoted there will increase over time and it can be seen as a small step towards a fully computerised price information system. Indeed, Harvard Securities has been considering a tele-broking system whereby people connected to Prestel could actually place buy and sell orders based on the prices quoted. This could enable dealing to take place 24 hours a day and will be a further step towards automation.

A recent entrant to the OTC market is a company called OTC Information Systems PLC, which has been established in order to provide a consistent, centralised and realistic price information system for the market-place. This is an important step forward in terms of published information and may herald the first move towards a NASDAQ-type system being established in the United Kingdom.

One of the most important steps forward as regards information on OTC shares is the introduction of an Extel OTC service. Started in October 1984, this service will enable investors to obtain all the relevant information on OTC stocks quickly and efficiently. All the cards are, of course, prepared to the usual high standards of Extel and will become invaluable to investors interested in this area of investment. Of particular importance will be the news card, which will inform investors of recent developments in a company that they might otherwise have overlooked.

Investors interested in the OTC market should be particularly aware that shares are negotiable instruments, meant to be bought and sold. Any shrewed investor in a company will keep a close watch not only on the share price of that company, but also on the particular industry in which the company operates. By doing this he may well be able to spot developments before there is a sharp reaction in the markets.

As the market continues to expand, more and more information will need to be made available. The obvious answer is for the UK market to develop its information system along the same lines as the US market. However, computerisation is an expensive option. With the market in its infancy and individual market makers already drained of working capital through having to finance book positions, this development looks to be a number of years away.

3 Licensed dealers in securities

The main anomaly of the OTC market in the United Kingdom at present is the dealers themselves. There are 15 active licensed dealers making up the UK market but these include a mixture of dealers – some exclusively matching bargains, some always quoting two-way prices (i.e. jobbing) and others which do both. Similarly, participants in the market range from the rare 'blue-blood' institutions to the very small operation designed simply to effect transactions.

Licensed dealers in securities are effectively companies other than stockbrokers or jobbers which are licensed by the Department of Trade to carry on the business of dealing in securities. They may do this in any shares, quoted or unquoted, and may also act as an issuing house, being responsible for bringing companies to the market. Permission to deal comes in the form of a principal's licence, which must be renewed every year, and various requirements must be met before such a licence is granted. For example, information must be provided about the directors, controllers and managers of the company, its indemnity arrangements and external financing, the source of its business and the types of client with which it expects to deal. In addition, information concerning the company's structure, giving the number and functions of employees, internal rules and disciplinary procedures, is required.

A licence holder must also make a deposit of £500 to be lodged with the Supreme Court Judicature. The Department of Trade is the licensed dealers' governing body and a principal's licence can be revoked at any time. Should this happen, the holder can appeal; a tribunal of inquiry, whose members are appointed by the Lord Chancellor's Department and the Treasury, would hear any such case. There has been some criticism about inflexibility of available sanctions which may be used against an existing licence holder should there be serious misgivings concerning its conduct. At the moment, complete revocation of a licence is the sole remedy available to the Secretary of State. Certainly, in some circumstances, it may be desirable to have the option to suspend a licence immediately pending an investigation and this is something the regulatory powers will undoubtedly be looking at.

The main function of the market making dealer is to make a liquid market in the shares being traded and to ensure that two-way transactions are maintained for both buyers and sellers. What actually happens to a share price depends entirely on market sentiment. An individual dealer, like a jobber, needs to be highly sensitive to changes in supply and demand. If sellers predominate, the dealer will 'mark down' his prices until selling is deterred or until buyers start to appear, attracted by the lower prices. Alternatively, should demand rise then so will the price. The jobbing dealer usually buys and sells even though he has no corresponding buyers and sellers in sight with whom he can readily complete a trade. Obviously, a jobbing dealer may have a preference to sell or to buy but regardless of his preference he has to maintain a two-way market and must execute trades at the price he quotes.

In order that a two-way market is maintained, a dealer must be prepared to sell, and once the sale has been completed he must be able to deliver what he has sold. For this reason, a dealer will normally always hold a book position (see page 34) in all the stock that he trades. Thus, the dealer will buy and sell stock for his own account. The book position of active licensed dealers is likely to change frequently, particularly in the more popular issues. It is up to the judgement and skill of the dealer involved to decide the positions actually held.

When trading on the OTC, the dealer must follow closely all enquiries that he receives in respect of any security in which he makes a market. Increasingly, as stocks begin to have more than one market maker, dealers will ensure that the prices they quote are roughly in line with those of other market makers. If their quotes become uncompetitive, they will lose business. Further, if the prices quoted drift far enough apart, it is possible that backwardation may occur and the uncompetitive dealer will be forced to alter his prices to avoid being left with surplus stock on his books. Moreover, the dealer must keep in touch with current financial, economic and political news that may affect securities. He must also closely follow the market trends of the main exchange, since 'bull' and 'bear' cyclical trends do have a knock-on effect on the OTC market (see page 36).

Risk

One major element of difference between a licensed dealer (when acting as a principal) and a stockbroker in the United Kingdom is that the former bears a risk. A broker acts as an agent in that it buys and sells for the account and risk of the customer and naturally it does not possess an ownership interest in the securities which are bought and sold. On the other hand, a licensed dealer actually takes ownership of the securities that it sells as a principal. Obviously, because a licensed dealer is buying for its own account, it will seek to market the shares on its book as soon as possible and it is for this reason that the majority of licensed dealers employ a 'retail' sales force.

As it is not always possible to complete transactions immediately, the holding of a book position (or inventory, as it is sometimes referred to in the United States) can be seen as a necessity. But, while holding this 'inventory' of shares, the dealer, as the owner, assumes all the risks of a shareholder and puts its own capital at risk. However, this holding of stock does serve a purpose in that it acts as a buffer; the inventory both absorbs supply when demand is absent and releases stock from its book position when demand is not otherwise readily available. Sudden increases of supply over demand or of demand over supply (i.e. the normal market mechanism) are the most common causes of sharp price changes. A broker simply acting as an agent is in no position to remedy such a situation and by its recommendations may well even exacerbate the price movements. In contrast, dealers, buying and selling for their own account, tend to give some continuity and stability to the market in the issue in which they deal. By acting as intermediaries, dealers do tend to keep supply and demand in a more closely balanced relationship, serving to minimise price fluctuations. This is particularly important when, as in some OTC companies, the shares are traded very thinly. Thus, prices on the OTC are less volatile than those of new stocks issued in the early days of the USM.

Another way dealers help to maintain a more orderly and stabilised market is by actively undertaking to merchandise stock. Unlike brokers, dealers are not content simply to process buying and selling orders. Instead, through their sales department, licensed dealers attempt to convert active or even latent buying interest into actual demand. The market can be stimulated in this way through the medium of the telephone, which is, of course, the unifying element in the OTC market-place. By acting as a principal, the dealer can to some extent direct the market. This system, coupled with the NASDAQ (National Association of Securities Dealers Automated Quotations) computer surveillance methods, has proved to be very successful in the United States, albeit within the auspices of the SEC (Securities and Exchange Commission) and NASD (National Association of Securities Dealers). The UK market is perhaps too immature to allow sweeping statements to be made concerning performance but it has certainly proved to date to be less cyclical than the major markets.

Return

For providing this service as a principal holder of stock, the dealer must have some return. The holding of any securities involves a risk element and considerable capital is needed to finance a large book position. Unlike a stockbroker, a licensed dealer, when acting as a principal, does not charge commission. Therefore, a dealer's return comes from the spread it charges, i.e. the difference between the bid and offer prices. The nature of this charge is no different from an ordinary commercial transaction; any business must sell at a higher price than the cost or purchase price in order to make a profit on the deal. In the past it has been acknowledged that spreads have been too wide, although this is now changing. A recent report by the European Commission on Secondary Stock Markets states that the average spread quoted by Harvard Securities is around 10% and 'seems to be competitive with the spread of jobbers in comparable securities . . .'. Even so, large spreads do still occur in certain situations on OTC-quoted stocks. In fairness, USM spreads can also, at times, become very wide and the middle price of a share quoted in the *Financial*

Times may be substantially higher or lower than the actual dealing price. It is obvious that narrower spreads make trading more attractive to the investor and market makers must be made well aware of this.

Competition between different market makers does, as has been seen in the United States, effectively narrow the spread. As more market makers enter into OTC transactions, these spreads will become even tighter. Already, companies such as Hard Rock Cafe have three competing market makers. This type of competition can only be good for the market as a whole, since it increases the overall liquidity of an investor's holdings. Both BIDS and NASDIM have recognised this and the proposed changes to both sets of rule books will require that there are at least three market makers for each stock traded OTC. This is an example of how the OTC in the United Kingdom is looking to the US market for guidance, as in the NASDAQ system all major stocks must have at least four market makers.

The decision by the Inland Revenue to grant the so-called 'jobber's stamp'* concession to USM stocks could well mark the entry of a number of market makers, outside of The Stock Exchange, into unlisted securities trading. Previously, this concession, whereby jobbers paid only a nominal 50 pence transfer duty per transaction instead of the 1% standard rate, was a closely guarded preserve. Now that bodies such as licensed dealers outside the control of The Stock Exchange can compete on an equal footing there could be a substantial increase in the level of competition in the securities industry.

Bull and bear markets

The early rapid growth experienced by the OTC market in the United Kingdom has been achieved during the occurr-

* See s.42, Transfer Stamp Act 1920, as amended by s.100. Transfer Stamp Act 1980.

ence of a major 'bull' market (due to the favourable political climate) on the main exchanges. Critics of the OTC therefore claim that its success is based on the upward surges of the established markets and that calamity will strike when a major 'bear' market appears. This pessimistic viewpoint fails to acknowledge the quality of some of the companies traded OTC.

The market as it stands at the moment has grown too large to be simply a product of the prevailing bull market and it will not, as many people claim, disappear overnight. Although 'bull' and 'bear' trends are important, the cyclical effects of the stock market are actually lessened on the OTC, mainly because the market is in all senses distanced from the main exchanges. There are a number of reasons for this. First, the predominantly private-client base of the OTC is likely to react more quickly to any significantly bad news than, say, a large institution. Second, the 'herd-like' instinct of the major institutions is such that if one of them decided to sell it is likely they will all sell and the aggregate effect of this would be severely felt on a market dominated by this type of investment. And third, as mentioned earlier, the existence of stockbrokers, interested primarily in turnover, may well even exacerbate cyclical movements, since their buy and sell recommendations can cause either shortages or surpluses of supply. The market maker which actually holds a position in all the stocks it deals in can counter sudden surges in supply and demand and create a more orderly and stable market. This is something critics of a dual-capacity system could do well to consider.

Nevertheless, a major bear market would have an appreciable 'knock-on' effect on the OTC, as individual investors observing events on the major markets decided to liquidate their equity holdings. If and when this does occur, the fact that some of the market-making firms are under capitalised could well be exposed. The weakness of the capital structure, compared to the turnover that some dealers are at the present time attaining, is critical. In order to continually quote a bid and offer price in a company's shares, especially if trading volume is low, a dealer must have a fairly wide capital base. This is because it is occasionally necessary for dealers to take quite large positions in some of the shares they quote.

Obviously, in any bear market the positions that dealers have to take increase and the consequent drain on working capital may cause severe cash-flow problems. There are those who feel that at its present state of development the market is strong enough to cope with the failure of one of the main trading market makers. However, if one looks to the United States for guidelines, the Denver OTC provides a classic example of how a fast-growing market, based on a strong bull trend and undercapitalised market-making firms, can collapse. The danger signs are clearly there and, in spite of efforts to increase capital bases, formal or more effective self-regulation is becoming increasingly necessary.

With the City changing fast, the way seems clear for the OTC to develop into a major market for raising equity capital. The meteoric rise in the size and status of the OTC market in the United States over a relatively short period of time bodes well for the development of the UK market. So far, it has raised around £80 million for UK industry and created 6,000 new jobs, therefore playing a crucial role in the regeneration of the UK economy.

4 An OTC quote – the benefits and costs for companies

The OTC market in the United Kingdom has never been very clearly defined and, in fact, the term itself in many quarters is used as a blanket phrase covering all unlisted stocks not dealt with on The Stock Exchange. This is not strictly true, however, and the market is now establishing itself as a major 'third-tier' route to equity finance. The whole market-place has attracted considerable criticism already, being labelled as a 'spiv's paradise' and generally being frowned upon by the established stock markets.

The traditional Stock Exchange view is that only substantial mature companies should be able to gain a public listing; small and high-risk companies should gradually establish an institutional-shareholder base and should not go public before their high-risk profile characteristics fade. This implies that there should be no secondary market for small companies and that they should therefore raise their equity privately. However, many entrepreneurs strongly resent the high level of outside influence that comes with private capital raising and prefer public equity issues.

However, on the main stock markets it is quite possible for a large percentage of the company's shares to be placed in 'unfriendly' hands. Furthermore, because of the institutional dominance of the major exchanges, it is quite normal for listed companies to have just a few major shareholders, who may well have the power to exert unwelcome influence on the management. But on the OTC market, because institutional involvement is minimal, it is very rare for there to be a major external shareholder. Typically there is a large number of small private investors, who are individually unable to influence either management policy or the share price.

In practice, The Stock Exchange wishes to guard its reputation and shies away from bringing high-risk companies to the market. Certainly, the prestige of a stock market is based on the proficiency of the market organisation and on the quality of the companies that have their shares traded on it. For example, the New York Stock Exchange chooses to maintain a very high threshold of quality and to leave it up to other market segments to cater for the needs both of smaller companies and of investors seeking investment with a greater degree of risk. The OTC, as a 'third tier', can cater well for such high-risk companies and for such investors. Those companies who come to the OTC may well have found other avenues, such as increased debt finance, closed to them. Therefore, the sole form of finance for expansion and development may well involve selling off a certain percentage of equity on the OTC.

Undoubtedly, there will be a rise in demand for equity finance, as companies emerging from the recession need to invest more and as progressive reductions in corporation tax (as announced in the 1984 Budget) even out the previous bias in favour of debt finance, which arose due to the fact that interest payments are tax deductible, whereas dividends are not.

The benefits of an OTC quote

The OTC market operates under the basic principle of providing marketability for a company's shares and being able to obtain this more cheaply, with less complication and with far greater speed than that experienced in the major public markets. The other major benefits of an OTC quote can be listed as follows:

1 The OTC can provide a company with equity finance at a far earlier stage in its development than if it were to go through the traditional company financing route.
2 A company with marketable securities to offer as consideration has the means by which it can make acquisitions using paper instead of cash. Moreover, under legislation in force since January 1980, shares are considerably more acceptable to vendors than cash, since a share exchange does not give rise to capital gains tax liability.
3 An OTC quote will avoid the publicity and higher profile that now comes as part and parcel of any flotation on The Stock Exchange. Thus, pressure from the financial press is alleviated and the scrutiny of the public is avoided.
4 The OTC provides an ideal nurturing ground for small, private companies to adjust to the rigours of 'public' life and to become familiar with events such as an Annual General Meeting.
5 The dominance of private investors on the OTC ensures a greater spread of shareholders, thus reducing the possibility of a predator building up a stake and launching a take-over bid.
6 The structure of the market is such that most licensed dealers always hold a line of stock in the shares in which they make a market. Therefore, it can offer a greater degree of price stability, due to the fact that the dealer is

holding stock as a buffer, and can absorb temporary
price fluctuations.

7   A company using the OTC is faced with one single
source of financial expertise in the shape of a licensed
dealer. Nearly all management teams involved in any
type of flotation find it a very time-consuming, complex
and, at times, confusing exercise. As such, the fewer
people involved at the outset the better. A licensed
dealer, in its role as an issuing house, will offer a
complete package to a potential OTC candidate.
Furthermore, the whole deal can be put together and a
prospectus produced in a relatively short space of time.

At the moment at Harvard Securities, any prospectus will be
prepared to the standard of The Stock Exchange 'yellow
book' (i.e. those requirements which have to be fulfilled in a
prospectus by a company obtaining a 'full' quote on The
Stock Exchange) as, in the absence of any statutory body to
vet prospectuses, this offers the best guidelines. Indeed, the
contents of the prospectus of any OTC company are
governed by a combination of the requirements laid down
by The Stock Exchange (which, although not applicable to
the OTC, are usually adhered to by licensed dealers) and the
Companies Act 1948. The prospectus serves both as a legal
document and as a marketing document and these,
sometimes contradictory, elements have to be reconciled,
since the directors have a statutory duty to ensure that the
prospectus is true, accurate and not misleading.

There are other advantages of an OTC quote, too.
Because of the existence of a continuous, two-way market,
the shares have a properly determined value, which may be
useful should there be any capital gain or death duty
liabilities. A major problem for all small family businesses
or partnerships is that, should one member wish to retire,
the other directors may be faced with a severe cash-flow
problem if they have to 'buy out' the person intending to

retire. With shares that are readily marketable, this problem does not arise.

As with all public flotations, the status of the company is enhanced. Both debtors and creditors seem more prepared to do business with a 'PLC'. The same is true of banks, which are more willing to lend to a public quoted company. A comment frequently heard from directors whose company has gone public is that, suddenly, people are making them offers of finance! Without doubt, a public quote will provide enhanced access to capital markets. Once an initial flotation has taken place, a company can, of course, return to the OTC for a secondary placing or a rights issue (an invitation to existing shareholders to acquire additional shares, usually at a lower price than on the open market).

A typical timetable for a company to be floated on the OTC can be seen in Appendix II. Although a tremendous work-load is placed on the management of a company during the course of a flotation, all the work necessary is of great use to the company once it has achieved 'public' status. From this point of view, the OTC is a good springboard for companies aspiring to the USM. With much of the initial 'spadework' done, transition costs may be low, and, since the company will have experienced some of the rigours of life as a 'listed' company, it may be better prepared for full, public company status when the time arises.

The costs of an OTC quote

Now that the benefits of obtaining long-term finance via the OTC market have been discussed in some detail, it is necessary to outline the associated costs.

1 One intangible disadvantage often aired is that OTC shares are unlisted. Their lower status and degree of marketability combine with their high-risk nature to

provide a somewhat lower price for the shares. Thus, there is an opportunity cost to the company that may result from an underpricing of the shares at the initial flotation. This may mean that the net worth and degree of liquidity of a company on the OTC market is less than if it had been quoted on a more recognised public exchange. However, the degree of liquidity on the USM sometimes leaves a lot to be desired, with prices of stocks that are thinly traded frequently being 'basis' only (see page 20). Moreover, to cite liquidity as a major problem is to misunderstand the role of the OTC. Companies which come to the OTC do so usually because they are too young or too small for the USM or The Stock Exchange. As a third-tier route to equity finance, the market is not in competition with either USM or full-listed status and, as such, comparisons of liquidity between markets are not valid. However, it is fair to say that, as a high-risk market, some discount in the price of the shares traded OTC is usually unavoidable.

2   Because of the necessary disclosure requirements, any sort of public listing may be unsuitable if a company is involved in a very competitive field. For example, if it is developing a product that depends upon technological advances to keep it ahead of competition, being in the gaze of both the press and the public may be disadvantageous in commercial terms.

3   A more obvious disadvantage of an OTC quote is the cost involved. The cost of a public share quotation per unit of capital raised is a good deal higher for small companies than for large ones. As a result, it may be uneconomic for certain smaller companies to raise equity. This is not to say that the activities which give rise to listing costs are wasteful, however. Essentially, they are intended to benefit the issuing company. Nevertheless, the benefit derived in some situations may

not balance the cost. The principal costs involved in a placing are the dealer's commission (which includes the cost of underwriting), external accountants' and solicitors' fees and producing and printing the prospectus, as well as the costs of the company's own professional advisers.

The OTC, therefore, is not a cheap method of obtaining finance and, since the listing and prospectus requirements, as laid down by BIDS, must be adhered to by all members, the expenses of disclosure are high. Corporate disclosure facilitates the valuation of capital raising instruments and, as such, is essential information for potential investors. It seems that the best way to reduce the cost of disclosure is to increase competition among the licensed dealers offering this facility. It is for this very reason that no attempt should be made to fit licensed dealers into either the banking system or the Stock Exchange system. They must be allowed to compete and should on no account be absorbed into existing market systems.

In the light of all this any company considering equity finance must first weigh up the advantages and disadvantages of using the OTC rather than other methods of finance. Occasionally, private venture capital raised with the aid of stockbrokers or merchant banks, without the direct and indirect costs associated with the OTC, may be more appropriate.

Companies suitable for an OTC quote

As already stressed throughout this chapter, the OTC is the lowest market segment of the equity financing structure. As such, it deals with young, exciting companies as well as possible start-up situations.

However, it must be borne in mind that there must be some quality control on companies seeking finance.

Investors and the volume of their funds committed to the OTC are the life-blood of the market-place and, because of this, a licensed dealer must guard, to a certain extent, the reputation of the companies in which it trades. A string of company failures would result in investors moving away from the market and looking, instead, at other investment opportunities.

When a proposal is first put to a licensed dealer, its corporate finance department must satisfy itself on a number of points. Increasingly, companies to be floated on the OTC must have some sort of track record; it is very difficult to make an accurate profit forecast on a start-up project. This is not to say, however, that a well-researched and well-presented greenfields project would not be accepted by a licensed dealer as an OTC candidate, but a 12-month trading record would receive a much warmer reception. More importantly, business prospects must be good and there should be a reasonable diversification of markets, a wide range of customers and a number of sources of supply. The company must not be at the height of its business cycle and there should be a good deal of mileage left in both product and markets. In addition, the company must not be about to introduce a product which may completely change the nature of its business, invalidating its previous trading record.

The financial requirements of the company must be on a sound base and its capital structure should be relatively straightforward. In particular, if it is to qualify for the Business Expansion Scheme, there must not be partially owned subsidiaries. Finally, the company must have sufficient depth of management and key personnel.

In considering a flotation, there are also a number of important timing considerations which must be borne in mind. The audited figures given in the prospectus must not be more than six months old by yellow book standards (i.e. for a full Stock Exchange quote) and not more than nine months old for a USM quote. A licensed dealer will normally take either of these figures when looking at an OTC flotation. If the flotation takes place too near a company's year-end this could well prohibit a meaningful profit forecast and usually, unless there are pressing requirements for the float to take place, this would be avoided.

As far as the issuing house is concerned, there are certain times of the year when it may be prohibitive, due to the state of the general markets, to float a company on the OTC. For example, the markets can be pretty lifeless at certain periods in the summer and, for obvious reasons, an entry on to the market during the Christmas period would not be very well received. But at the end of the day, it is up to the licensed dealer to promote the issue and sell the shares. In many cases the dealer will underwrite the issue and so the final timing decision will be left in its hands as it is in the best position to take account of market sentiment.

Management support

In most OTC floated companies the management need support during the first two or three years after the input of new finance. Most OTC market makers have hitherto adopted a hands-off (i.e. no involvement with the company management or company objectives) management policy, however, although it is now becoming increasingly necessary to provide some early assistance for these new companies.

Obviously, the level of care varies from company to company but the minimum appears to be semi hands-off (reviewing management information on a monthly basis, for example, and having regular discussions with company management) with, in exceptional cases, full hands-on management where the licensed dealer becomes involved in the day-to-day running of the company. This type of management commitment by a licensed dealer cannot be expected to last long, however, since the cost of retaining a significant corporate finance department able to cope with these types of problem is prohibitive. The best a licensed dealer can offer is to use the full hands-on approach until alternative or additional management can be found. From the licensed dealer's point of view, it would be preferable not to get involved with the management of companies floated. Licensed dealers hands are full enough coping with the corporate finance and professional work required to take a company onto the public markets, raising finance for the company and, after the flotation, market making without having to get involved in the day-to-day running of companies.

If hands-on management became necessary in a large number of instances, a licensed dealer might need to review the minimum requirements it lays down for companies wishing to obtain a flotation. Obviously, a company which has been in existence for three or four years will be better able to handle new funds than one which has only a one- or two-year trading record. It would be a pity if very young companies or start-ups could not obtain funding, however, since the OTC market, together with the Business Expansion Scheme, should be able to cater for this type of company.

In companies which have short-term difficulties, the first course of action is to provide finance to support the business until the necessary changes have been made to make the company profitable again. When private investors are involved, it is possible to arrange for new shares to be purchased at a significant discount to the share price, which will satisfy the immediate cash requirement. However, shares purchased in this way cannot usually be sold for, say, six months. This exercise enables the licensed dealer to negotiate long-term finance via a rights issue – this should also be completed at a deep discount (to significantly dilute the equity of the errant directors) and preferably qualify for BES relief.

Independent accountants should be appointed to investigate the company's problems and to establish the extent of its weaknesses. Long-term management changes and, possibly, changes in the control of the company will be required, but to achieve these with the co-operation of existing directors requires considerable negotiating capabilities and time.

The directors themselves often need to be extensively investigated, particularly the financial director, and controls on the use of funds may need to be put into operation. For example, company cars and directors' salaries are obvious areas where excessive spending can occur. It is important that directors' salaries are kept as low as possible, certainly below £25,000 per annum, with the bulk of any salary being made up out of profits-related earnings, since most new issues are floated on a forecast-profit basis. The refinancing of a company is not an excuse to waste money, especially not at the immediate post-inflation stage. New capital should be used carefully and cautiously to develop and expand business and to justify the confidence and faith of new investors – expensive cars and high salaries are permissible only when a company has achieved its forecast profits.

The OTC market is still relatively small, and so companies raising funds should take care not to flood the market with paper. The market will tolerate initial fund raising of around £1 million, with a rights issue in the second or third year of not more than 50% of the initial funding. Public relations is an important area to be considered by the new company but in all probability the licensed dealer will advise and ensure that as much information as possible is made public. In recent years complaints from shareholders in OTC companies have centred around lack of information. It is therefore important that new companies on the OTC keep their shareholders informed. With the service provided by Extel and *OTC-I*, and with *OTC Magazine*, the *USM/OTC Review*, *Financial Weekly* and other financial-press monitoring, this complaint should not arise in the future.

5 Regulation of the OTC industry

Any substantial development of the OTC market in the United Kingdom must be accompanied by a commensurate development of regulations to protect investors. Establishing investor confidence is, of course, vital to the functioning of any securities market but in a high-risk market such as the OTC, which is particularly vulnerable to scandal, it is of paramount importance. If a private investor is to be encouraged to put his money into the small, high-risk company which is the life-blood of the OTC, he must be convinced that the market is legitimately 'policed' by an effective and independent body.

It is vital that a proper regulatory framework for the OTC is worked out as soon as possible. Any well-publicised case of investors losing out due to malpractice on the part of a dealer would be certain to deter both current and potential OTC investors. Undoubtedly, it would be a serious set-back if the potential of the market was harmed because of a scandal in the early years. Dealing must not only be fair; it must also be widely seen to be fair. If there are any cases of incompetent or fraudulent dealings, the offending dealers must be effectively disciplined and there must be adequate compensation for any injured parties. Once these measures are put into effect, the public must be made well aware of their existence so that confidence in the market is fostered. This point is especially pertinent, since hostility from conventional financial circles towards the OTC is now beginning to subside and the time seems right for the market to build on its growing legitimacy.

Apart from the Department of Trade's control over the issue of licences, there is no formal mechanism at all for regulating the market-place. At present the market's operation depends upon the 'integrity and efficiency of the firms and companies concerned' (Gower Report, page 144) and not on any formal regulations other than the Licensed Dealers (Conduct of Business) Rules 1983. The OTC in the United States has grown entirely within the strict regulatory framework of both the SEC and NASD and, if the UK market is to become established as a major market-place for young, aspiring public companies, the degree of regulation in the United Kingdom must be upgraded along the lines of that practised in the United States. There are a number of points about the US market which are especially worthy of note. First, many small companies in the United States go public during their first or second year. Second, Regulation A of the SEC provides reduced disclosure requirements for small-company issues of up to $1.5 million per annum and permits public issues on the basis of unaudited financial statements. Third, Regulation D permits small companies to issue shares of up to $0.5 million per annum to the public without any disclosure document. Finally, some 20,000 companies in the United States enjoy what is effectively a secondary market for their securities, in which they do not have to meet the normal SEC disclosure requirements. Thus, recognition has been made in the United States of the value of a public issue of equity for small companies at an early stage in their development. It is, indeed, a vital component of any equity financing system that provisions are made to include companies that are young, small and highly risky. Everything which happens in the United States as a matter of course, such as the vetting of prospectuses, effective protection of investors and checks on liquidity and on the size of market positions, must become part of the OTC in the United Kingdom.

Major problems will arise if the market is allowed to run completely unchecked. The first problem which must be dealt with is the concentration of power which lies in the hands of licensed dealers. This is brought about by the fact that it is licensed dealers which bring companies to the market. They arrange the deal and the terms, too, and draft the prospectus. Dealers will also place the shares with their clients and act as agents in subsequent deals as well as making a market in the shares. Furthermore, they may well act as financial advisers on a continuing basis. In short, they are stockbroker, jobber and merchant bank all rolled into one.

Indeed, this power can only increase further as the market develops and as dealers bring more and more companies to the market. The pace at which the market is currently growing makes it imperative that some sort of regulatory framework is put into effect. This work is already, in part, under way, with both the British Institute of Dealers in Securities (BIDS) and the National Association of Securities Dealers and Investment Managers (NASDIM) working to establish themselves as the major self-regulatory bodies of the OTC market. There will be further discussion of these two bodies and of the advantages of self-regulation in the OTC market later in this chapter.

With the current climate of change in the City, future regulation of all the UK securities markets is, as yet, undecided and all kinds of complex proposals have been put forward by a number of interested parties. It is not within the scope of this book to explore in depth the prevailing arguments concerning the best way to control the delicate balances present in the sophisticated financial system of the United Kingdom. However, the fundamental conflicts which face legislators at the present time are extremely relevant when considering regulation of the OTC market. These can be neatly summarised into two main areas.

1   In supervising and controlling the issue of securities to the general public, should they adopt the attitude that the man on the street ought to be able to look after himself in evaluating investment proposals (i.e. *caveat emptor*), or should he be protected by the State?
2   Having decided how much protection needs to be accorded to the public, the legislators then have to decide how this protection is to be enforced. Is there a need for strict legislation, which would have to be laid before Parliament before going on to the statute-book? Alternatively, would enforcement of regulations be better achieved through a self-regulatory agency, which would be set up, administered and regulated by people working in their respective industry and which, in theory, would be able to control its members more effectively?

Whatever is finally decided, it will almost certainly be some sort of compromise between these two main areas of conflict. If discipline is to be effective but at the same time not stifle activity, it must to a large extent be in the hands of people close to the markets, who fully appreciate their operation. However, regulation should ultimately rest on the authority of the law, so that meaningful sanctions can be imposed.

One important point that legislators must not overlook when considering mechanisms to administer investor protection is that external factors can and do serve to regulate the financial services industry. For example, competition between dealers in the market will mean that the services offered by the City will become more adapted to consumers' needs and more responsive to their criticisms. Also, a free flow of good-quality information, which information technology is at present helping to disseminate, will aid investors and educate more people in the methods of the stock markets as well as removing some of the mystique extended by The Stock Exchange.

However, it is important to bear in mind that the basic function of the OTC market is to provide access to equity finance for small, young and high-risk companies. While greater disclosure of information and stricter control over the whole market-place is desirable, it is far too easy to get carried away with the notion that strict regulations are wholly suitable. Although a tightening of control in specific areas, such as safeguarding clients' accounts and measures against high-pressure selling, 'churning' and creating a false market, will be to the benefit of everybody, entry to the market must not be impeded by minimum requirements as to age, size and intrinsic risk, nor by high entry costs. Efforts to regulate the market, however, may well involve an upgrading of the entry requirements for small companies, as increased disclosure requirements come to bear. It should be recognised that the quality of disclosure of a young company markedly increases as its trading record lengthens and there is a real danger that if strict disclosure requirements are imposed the public issue of small, young companies may well be inhibited. This, in turn, will effectively grant to institutional investors the privilege of exclusively funding small companies in their early formative years.

Obviously, stricter disclosure would also escalate the costs associated with public issues. This would increase the size and, therefore, the age that a company must reach before it could economically raise equity capital by a public issue. If this were allowed to happen, equity would once more become the domain of the mature, established company.

The current legal framework

During the 1920s and 1930s, the selling of worthless securities in the United Kingdom by fraudulent and unscrupulous dealers became widespread. With no form of investor protection whatsoever, so-called 'share pushers' sold worthless shares in imaginary companies to an unsuspecting public. Furthermore, they often induced clients to deposit cash with them for discretionary investment purposes (see page 3). A client's hard-earned money, along with the promoter concerned, was all too prone to vanish and, with no statutory regulations, this became a common occurrence. Since investors provided such easy prey, 'share pushing' became almost epidemic, one scandal following the next. Indeed, the situation became so bad that the Board of Trade was forced to set up two committees to consider how best to tackle the problem. The Anderson Committee on Fixed Trusts (1936) and the Bodkin Committee on Share Pushing (1937) both sought to impose some sort of regulation on the equity market-place and led to the Prevention of Fraud (Investments) Act.

The Prevention of Fraud (Investments) Act 1939 sought to terminate the activities of fraudulent dealers by forbidding persons from carrying on the business of dealing in securities unless:

(a) they were authorised to do so by licence and so were known as licensed dealers; or

(b) they were exempt from obtaining such a licence because they fell within certain categories of persons specified in the Act; these included members of The Stock Exchange, any recognised association of dealers in securities, the Bank of England or any statutory corporation.

However, once a licence had been obtained, the statutory requirements were not onerous. The main idea was to bring everybody under the umbrella of The Board of Trade and to use revocation of the licence as the ultimate sanction.

The Prevention of Fraud (Investments) Act 1958 is largely a re-enactment of the 1939 Act. A number of amendments have been made from time to time but there have been no substantial revisions of the Act, which is, therefore, still designed to deal with the problems that arose from the financial practices of the 1930s. The need to update the Act was particularly highlighted in the report of the Company Law Committee, chaired by Lord Jenkins in 1962. This report pin-pointed the major areas of concern as follows:

1   The range of occupations covered by the provision of the Act for licensed dealers needs to be widened.
2   Fuller information should be required from applicants for licences.
3   There should be provisions for suspension as well as revocation of licences.
4   Restrictions on invitations to the public to investment, whether in the form of circulars or advertisements or in other ways, should be strengthened and the activities of agents of overseas companies brought within the Act.
5   The financial penalties laid down in the Act and the deposit to be paid by licence holders should both be increased.

None of these recommendations, though valid, has yet been put into practice. Indeed, in spite of much rhetoric, little or nothing has actually been done to improve supervision of this particular area of the securities market.

It is under the Prevention of Fraud (Investments) Act that

the rules which govern licensed dealers are made. Under section 7 of the Act, the Board of Trade (or the Department of Trade and Industry, as it has now become) '. . . may make rules for regulating the conduct of holders of licences . . .' This they have done, in the form of statutory instruments duly authorised by the Act, which seek to regulate the conduct of business of dealing in securities. Although backed up by statutory provisions, these rules, which related only to dealings in stocks and shares, still proved to be ineffective and related badly to the market-place they were supposed to regulate.

During 1980 and 1981 there were a number of well-publicised cases which highlighted the inadequacies of the rules governing licensed dealers, the collapse of the discretionary investment manager, Norton Warburg, being perhaps the best known example. There has since been a number of failures, including M. L. Doxford, Signal Life and Connaught Latham. As a result, in 1981 the Department of Trade announced that a wide ranging review of investor protection was to be conducted by Professor Laurence Gower, with a view to replacing, in due course, the 1958 Act. In the mean time it proposed to update the Licensed Dealers' (Conduct of Business) Rules 1960, which, as explained above, are issued by the Secretary of State with the powers conferred in the 1958 Act. The new Licensed Dealers' Rules are contained in Statutory Instrument 1983 No. 585 and deal specifically with a number of areas, including the following. First, they determine the manner and circumstances in which a licensed dealer may deal in securities and include provisions relating to client money and investments. Second, they prescribe the books, accounts and other documents which must be kept by the holder of a principal's licence and they require the holder of a licence to comply with generally accepted standards of good market practice.

While these new rules must be welcomed, they can really

be seen only as a stopgap measure. It is the Act itself which requires revision. It is understood that moves by the Department of Trade are afoot which will lead to widespread changes, but these have, so far, been delayed until consultations in the wake of the Gower Report are completed.

The Gower Report

The first and main part of Professor Gower's report gives his analysis and recommendations and the second part, which is to follow, will be a draft parliamentary bill giving effect to the recommendations. Briefly, the report outlines how the rules of the City and its structure should be altered, so that better protection is offered to both the private and the professional investor. The basic framework of the 212-page report is a recommendation for the establishment of a mixture of statutory and self-regulation. A new Investor Protection Act would replace the current Prevention of Fraud (Investments) Act and the new law would be administered by either a strengthened section of the Department of Trade or a self-standing commission, which would be answerable to the Secretary of State. The main implication of this Act will be that any person carrying on investment business will have to register either with the Department of Trade (or Commission) or with a number of recognised self-regulatory agencies (SRAs). In his interim report Professor Gower originally suggested that there should be as few as four SRAs, but subsequently, in response to the proposals in the report, as many as 18 or 20 such agencies have been put forward. It will be advantageous to keep the number of such agencies down, however, in order to prevent the proliferation of small, financially weak bodies, which may be unable to control their members effectively. In order to gain recognition, all agencies would be required to establish compensation funds similar to that currently operated by The Stock Exchange. All of these regulatory agencies would be represented on a strengthened Council for the Securities Industry (CSI), which would act in conjunction with the Department of Trade and Industry.

The report has all kinds of complex and controversial features, reflecting the complicated and tangled web of regulations. This has come about because of the present mixture of statutory and self-imposed restrictions, which, as Professor Gower points out, has resulted in 'a regulatory system which is difficult to enforce effectively'. In the main body of the report little is said about the OTC market directly. While acknowledging the inadequacies of the Licensed Dealers' Rules, it indicates that, at present, the market is fairly insubstantial. However, it does recognise the potential of the OTC and believes that it will experience considerable growth towards the end of the five-year period for which qualifying shares must be held in order to gain the tax advantages of the Business Expansion Scheme. Because of this, it states that there is a clear need for more effective regulations and that the vetting of original prospectuses should be regarded as being just as important, in terms of regulation, as control over share dealings. Company law in the United Kingdom requires a prospectus to be produced for the public marketing of shares. The report argues that the CSI, the Take-over Panel and The Stock Exchange should assume responsibility for vetting those prospectuses of companies wishing to sell securities other than through The Stock Exchange. Indeed, due to the rise in OTC flotations, Gower states that it is vital that the pre-vetting of prospectuses becomes mandatory.

Furthermore, he believes that the Prevention of Fraud (Investments) Act is both harmful and misleading. The main reason he cites for holding this view is that the Act, albeit unwittingly, draws a distinction between licensed dealers, who are subject to strict regulations, and the various exempted classes of dealers, who are subject to hardly any. The unfortunate result of this is that there is a stigma attached to the status of licensed dealers. Not surprisingly, being regulated by an Act entitled 'Prevention of Fraud', has meant that licensed dealers have, in the past, been regarded as fringe operators with a somewhat shady trading record.

Indeed, the Act can be seen to have equally bad side-effects when considering the position of the uninitiated investor. The fact that a dealer has actually been licensed by the Government to carry on the business of trading in securities may give an inexperienced investor the impression that the company concerned has in some way been approved by the Government, the licence being a sign of respectability and reliability. Neither of these impressions is necessarily correct. Indeed, each must be regarded as misleading and unfair to investors and dealers alike.

Self-regulatory agencies (SRAs)

The City has for some time argued that self-regulation, rather than governmental control, is the ideal way to police the financial community. Self-regulation will undoubtedly play a major role in the future supervision of the financial activities of the United Kingdom, particularly as the Gower Report recommends this type of agency to be set up in order to provide supervision of the securities industry.

Certainly, self-regulation has a number of advantages over Governmental supervision. Practitioners will have direct experience of the particular market concerned and therefore ought to be able to regulate it more sensitively and effectively than would civil servants. Also, a self-regulatory body is able to lay down flexible codes of conduct rather than rigid legal requirements, which would facilitate interpretation of the spirit of the law and thus allow quick reactions to any change in circumstances. Since these agencies would cover only a small area of the investment business, bureaucracy would probably not take over and begin to strangle the free workings of the market-place. The SEC (Securities and Exchange Commission) in the United States is a good example of what could happen if the Government opted for centralised, statutory control. The SEC has been described as 'a bureaucratic, lawyer-ridden monster' which creates mountain-loads of paperwork for all concerned. It is essential that a legalistic strait-jacket, which would inevitably fetter and restrain the initiative and spirit vital to keep London at the forefront of the world's financial markets, is not imposed. In fact, the general mood of the City is against the establishment of any general commission along the lines of the SEC, although there are dangers with self-regulation, too. This type of agency can become very inward looking and tends to act in favour of members and against the interests of the general public. The Stock Exchange is itself a self-regulatory body, but, until the authorities successfully pushed for a number of radical changes in the structure of the Exchange, it was extremely narrow-minded, behaving like an exclusive gentleman's club.

In order that these agencies prove worth while, however, they will have to satisfy some stiff conditions. They will need detailed rule books and stringent entry qualifications for potential members. Furthermore, they will require some monitoring and disciplinary procedures in order to keep members in line. Finally, they will need to show that they can offer protection to investors against mismanagement, which will in most cases take the form of insurance schemes or compensation funds.

At present, there are two major bodies concerned with non-statutory regulation in the securities market, the Take-over Panel and the Council for the Securities Industry (CSI). The Take-over Panel was set up in 1968 as a result of widespread criticism of some of the practices adopted in the take-over 'battles' of the 1960s. In essence, it exists to interpret and administer the City code on take-overs and mergers and includes representatives from merchant banking, stockbroking, legal and accounting backgrounds and an independent chairman and deputy chairman appointed by the Governor of the Bank of England.

The present code applies to offers for all public companies, whether listed or not, and the panel's main objective is to see that bids are fairly conducted. As such, it is not particularly concerned about the merits of any specific bid, its aim being simply to ensure that shareholders are given adequate information and sufficient time to make a proper judgement. Day-to-day supervision of the code is the responsibility of the panel executive, which works closely with the Quotations Department of The Stock Exchange. A major problem is that the panel has no statutory backing and has no power to take evidence on oath or to subpoena documents or witnesses. The authority of the panel, therefore, rests on its general acceptance within the financial community, its main sanction being public censure.

The Council for the Securities Industry was set up in March 1978 and is the closest thing the City has to an overseer. Its main objective is to maintain high ethical standards within the securities industry. The CSI's activities, since it was set up, have included the drawing up of draft codes of conduct for dealers in securities. In May 1980 it produced a code of conduct for dealers in securities, which came into effect in August of the same year. However, like the Take-over Panel, it has no statutory powers and its authority comes from the commitment of the bodies it represents to support its activities and respect its rulings. As a whole it meets only four or five times a year and doubts have been expressed about the degree of power it has, its low level of staffing and its relationship with the bodies it represents (especially The Stock Exchange and the Issuing Houses Association). Criticisms are frequently made concerning the CSI, claiming that it has tried to cover too large an area and that, in doing so, it has failed to achieve sufficient credibility and practical usefulness. With a permanent staff of only two, this does seem to be almost inevitable. Professor Gower envisaged that the CSI would have a role as a kind of umbrella body, supervising the SRAs, but it is clear that it would have to be considerably strengthened in order for this to happen.

Although the Take-over Panel and the CSI have indirect supervisory power in the OTC market, there are two major self-regulatory bodies which have recently been established to monitor dealings in this market in particular. Both the National Association of Securities Dealers and Investment Managers (NASDIM) and the British Institute of Dealers in Securities (BIDS) are attempting to become the OTC's ruling body. It is certain that one of these will develop along the lines of the National Association of Securities Dealers (NASD), the voluntary, self-regulatory body which so effectively administers the OTC market in the United States.

NASDIM

The National Association of Securities Dealers and Investment Managers evolved from the Association of Licensed Dealers in Securities (ALDS), which was set up in 1979. It was felt that the potential client base of ALDS was too narrow, since it really only catered for licensed dealers in securities. In 1979, before the boom in the OTC, there were only a small number of firms holding licences to deal in securities and so, with backing from the Department of Trade and from the Bank of England, ALDS changed its constitution to include all firms which dealt in securities or practised investment management, and changed its name to NASDIM.

A major boost to NASDIM has been its formal recognition by the Secretary of State for Trade and Industry as a self-regulatory body under the provisions of the Prevention of Fraud (Investments) Act. In effect, this means that members of NASDIM will no longer have to apply to the Department of Trade for an annual licence to deal in securities. In future, members will be regulated by NASDIM itself, which will be responsible for investigating complaints and administering both disciplinary and admission procedures. This recognition, which took effect on 1 January 1984, has increased the popularity of NASDIM and in August 1984 it announced that membership had increased by some 45% to 427. NASDIM is also developing its constitution to include protective measures to safeguard the public. In October 1984 the first 'layer' of its insurance provisions against negligence, to cover professional indemnity, insurance and fidelity bonding for employees, became compulsory. Further moves, concerning the insurance of principals, are under way and should become effective soon. A rule book is also being put together, which would comprehensively regulate this particular section of the OTC.

NASDIM, although accepted in certain quarters as being the trade association for the OTC market, has a serious competitor in the shape of BIDS – a self-regulatory body aimed specifically at licensed dealers operating as market makers in the OTC.

BIDS

Although small in comparison to NASDIM (in terms of membership), the British Institute of Dealers in Securities is ideally placed to become the governing body for the OTC market, since all the major, active market makers, with the exception of Granville & Co. are affiliated to it. BIDS was set up in 1983 by the dealers themselves, convinced that their image would be considerably enhanced and investor confidence boosted by a governing, regulatory body which would oversee the activities of a new and growing market. It is the investor who is the most crucial element in any equity market; the number of investors and the volume of their funds committed to the market-place are critical to the success of the market. Therefore, BIDS has drawn up its own constitution and rule book covering both dealers and companies operating in the OTC. The central issues are the formation of a disciplinary committee, the requirements that every 'jobbing' market maker makes a market in a minimum of £250 worth of shares and that primary market makers endeavour to find a further two market makers in each share in which they make a market, and the establishment of a compensation fund insurance scheme to safeguard investors in the event of the financial collapse of any member. The BIDS compensation fund, financed by a levy placed on contract notes (up to a bargain value of £1,500 the levy is 30 pence, above £1,500 the levy is 65 pence), is gradually being built up to a substantial sum. Furthermore, it is hoped that this will soon be backed up by an insurance scheme, which will provide even greater protection. Future plans for BIDS include the establishment of a central clearing system, which could greatly speed up the receipt of share certificates by investors, a central information system and liquidity monitoring measures. Negotiations are also taking place to try to unify the market by having at least five market makers in every stock. This would introduce competition between market makers and so narrow the spread.

In effect, BIDS has taken over where the ALDS left off, in that it is an association consisting purely of licensed dealers, with all active market makers being represented. Obviously, the recognition of NASDIM by the Department of Trade has given it much credence, but many of its members have nothing at all to do with OTC operations. Instead, their interests range from insurance to discretionary portfolio management. In contrast, BIDS is exclusively concerned with the OTC market, covering by far the lion's share of the OTC's turnover, and is independently administered by its chairman, Roger Baden-Powell.

There is, therefore, an anomalous situation, whereby the largest and most widely accepted contender to become the major OTC trade association has little active interest in the OTC and no experience of market making, while the organisation which is ideally placed for this position is, as yet, unrecognised by the Department of Trade under section 15 of the 1958 Act.

BIDS will undoubtedly grow, however, and enjoy official recognition as more market makers emerge and seek specific self-regulation of their market-making activities. As well as providing regulation, BIDS offers members help in dealing with the regulations governing the industry and access to the substantial experience of its older members. It could be argued that BIDS and NASDIM should merge, with the BIDS chairman and committee controlling NAS-DIM's moves into these areas. In this way, BIDS members would no longer be under the direct control of the Department of Trade but the resultant body could claim to be wholly representative, containing all interested parties. However, in order for this to happen, NASDIM would have to alter some of its current regulations. For example, at present it is necessary to surrender one's principal's licence to become a member and, with NASDIM currently dominated by Granville & Co., other market makers are, not surprisingly, wary of such membership.

In conclusion, it is necessary to point out that the future supervision of the City is not a straightforward choice between self-regulation and statutory contol. To believe that this is so would be a serious misconception, as the choices are much more subtle than that. Any system of self-regulation must have some sort of recognition in statute. In the United States the self-regulatory body, NASD, is supported by the SEC and a similar sort of situation will have to prevail in the United Kingdom. Because of this any Investor Protection Act would need to recognise the SRAs that are created, so that they are able to fulfil their designated roles, and it will also need to include sanctions against them. Furthermore, the Secretary of State must hold some degreee of power over the SRAs, possibly through some statutory agency. In particular, the Secretary of State would be concerned with the composition of the ruling committees and the appointment of lay members. He must also have the authority to alter the rules of any such agency and even occasionally to force an agency to adopt a particular policy. The division between self-regulatory independence and Government intervention may become blurred at this stage but it is necessary for both forms of regulation to coexist and function harmoniously, so that the investor is protected as far as possible.

6 The Business Expansion Scheme

Purposes of the BES

For some time now there has been a fiscal bias in favour of government bonds, which has effectively reduced the attractiveness of equity investments. For example, UK gilt-edged securities held for more than a year are exempt from capital gains tax. Therefore, any measure which can be employed to counter such an imbalance and strengthen the base of investors who wish to participate in equity investment should be warmly welcomed. The Business Expansion Scheme (BES) is such a measure. This was originally introduced in the 1981 Budget as the Business Start-up Scheme, and the basic idea is to encourage equity investment by offering substantial tax incentives. In this way it was hoped that new businesses would be helped in their search for venture capital. The Business Start-up Scheme was, in fact, something of a failure. It was initially expected to create £200 million of new investment, but only approximately one-tenth of this figure was actually invested. As a result, the Government revised and amended the scheme in order to make it more attractive and the 1983 Finance Act brought about the introduction of the Business Expansion Scheme. Although very similar in concept, the BES embraces a much wider field and, importantly, includes established companies requiring finance in order to expand. Companies more than five years old are no longer excluded. Also, the maximum amount of relief available has doubled to more than £40,000 for each investor, provided he or she is a UK resident. This figure is available for each of the five years for which the scheme runs and so, in effect, an individual could gain relief on an investment totalling £200,000. The minimum investment still is, however, £500 per company.

The main aim of the scheme is to reduce the cost of high-risk equity investments in unquoted companies. This is achieved by granting tax relief at the taxpayer's top marginal rate of income tax (i.e. a maximum of 60%) paid in the tax year in which relief is applied for. Because the relief is extended at the highest rate on the amount invested in a qualifying company, the BES must rate as one of the most attractive tax shelters currently available. The scheme applies specifically to equity investment in unquoted companies and, as such, all companies listed either on the USM or on The Stock Exchange are excluded. Companies traded on the OTC market, however, are not excluded. Surely this must be seen as a Governmental seal of approval for the OTC market? Relief will be granted only on investments in fully paid shares and most companies are eligible for investment under the scheme as long as they carry on their business with a view to profit. Excluded companies are those involved in banking, leasing, dealing in stocks and shares and other financial services. The 1984 Budget also specifically excluded property development from BES participation, as widespread 'abuse' was occurring in this area.

The benefits of the BES are for external investors rather than for people putting money into their own business. As such, directors and employees are not eligible for relief. Indeed, relief will be denied to all those closely connected with the company in question. For the purposes of the scheme, 'closely connected persons' are all employees, paid directors and owners of 30% or more of the company's capital, including loan finance. Also excluded from the scheme are close family and business partners.

The BES is designed to promote new investment on a reasonably long-term basis. Thus, relief is obtainable only on new ordinary shares and is not granted on loan stock; nor is it granted on shares that carry any preferential rights to dividends, redemption or assets in a winding up. Investment in a company will still qualify for relief even if the company has wholly-owned subsidiaries, provided that these companies do themselves fall into the category of a qualifying company, as laid down in Schedule 5 of the 1983 Finance Act. Indeed, in such a case the holding company need not trade itself, provided that it has no other trading activity.

The scheme has been widely praised by the financial community for its innovative approach to encouraging investment in young high-risk companies and means that substantial relief is available for genuinely additional investment in unquoted companies. The BES therefore offers an opportunity for outside investors to involve themselves in the growth companies of the future at an early stage in their development, with the added attraction of a much reduced cost. Through the BES, the Government has clearly stated its recognition of the vital role new companies can play in the UK economy, particularly with regard to creating much-needed employment. Furthermore, by allowing companies traded on the OTC market to qualify it has indirectly provided a major shot in the arm for the OTC.

How the BES affects the OTC market

Schedule 5 of the 1983 Finance Act relates BES relief specifically to unquoted companies. Since companies whose shares are traded OTC are, for taxation purposes, classed as unquoted, an investment in an OTC quoted company, as long as this is undertaken at the time of the issue of the qualifying shares (i.e. provided that the shareholder is one of the original allottees), will be eligible for tax relief via the BES.

The developing OTC market, which caters almost exclusively for young, growing companies, is an ideal focal point for BES investments. Undoubtedly, the BES has added tremendously to the attractiveness of the companies coming to the market for finance. The high risks involved can be significantly countered by the tax relief available. So far, the scheme has proved to be a major success.

To encourage longer-term investments, the minimum period for which the investment must be held in order to qualify for relief is five years. This has helped the licensed dealers who provide a market for BES qualifying companies enormously, since the five-year holding period contributes to a much more stable and orderly market. The percentage of people who 'stag' an issue falls appreciably on a BES investment and the after-market is a good deal less hectic, as people are content to hold the shares as long-term investments.

By far the best way to gain the maximum advantage of a BES investment is through participation in an OTC flotation. However, much publicity has recently surrounded the various approved investment funds, which are, in effect, specialist funds assembled to invest moneys in qualifying businesses. These funds are approved by the Inland Revenue and will grant a certificate to participants allowing them to claim tax relief. This type of fund is usually managed by merchant banks, unit trust companies or venture capital institutions and is aimed at the private investor wishing to mitigate his tax liability. However, these funds do have a number of disadvantages which detract significantly from the benefits on offer. An investment in an approved fund is completely illiquid, only being realisable after the five-year 'holding' period. Should the investor face a cash constraint, it may be extremely difficult to liquidate the investment and extract the money. A qualifying investment through a licensed dealer provides a great deal more flexibility than an approved fund can offer. In this case, if an investor wishes to dispose of his BES investment within five years, this can easily be achieved by simply contacting the licensed dealer concerned. There will be some clawback of relief (the exact nature of any clawback has yet to be decided by the Inland Revenue), but in a case where there is an urgent need for liquid funds the ability to sell must be seen as a major advantage.

Any BES approved fund operates in a manner very similar to the orthodox unit trust, i.e. it uses investors' money to invest in a large number of companies. As well as reduced flexibility, the prospects of making large returns on investments are also reduced. Using an approved investment fund also denies the individual the opportunity to assess the merits of any particular investment. All portfolio decisions are taken by the management of the fund and the investor has no active participation at all. Concern is mounting, too, about the marketability of these companies once the five-year period has expired. Nobody quite knows how these funds propose to liquidate their clients' investments, but presumably some market-place for the shares must be found if the investors in the fund wish to sell. In addition, the administrative procedure for actually getting relief credited is not simplified by going through a fund. In the case of an investment via the OTC market it is the company secretary who provides the necessary form to obtain relief. In the case of a fund, however, the form is provided by the management.

The flexibility of a BES investment through the OTC cannot be over-emphasised. As mentioned above, such an investment can be quite easily liquidated, which means that the investor has the choice of either staying with the investment for the full five years or selling out at an earlier date. For the investor who is fast on his feet this can provide a useful opportunity; if the shares have moved up appreciably he can sell out, take the capital gain and then once again invest the principal sum in a qualifying investment, thereby maintaining his tax relief. Indeed, even if the investor is unable to maintain his relief intact because of timing problems, it may well be worth while to take a capital gain and simply pay off the tax clawback resulting from the sale of shares.

It is in this context that the major attractions of a BES investment are most apparent. By reducing the cost of the investment, the potential losses are mitigated. Thus, if the share price nosedives, the loss is to some extent subsidised by the tax relief and it may well recover over the five-year period. If, on the other hand, the share price should rise rapidly, because of the flexibility of BES/OTC investments, an investor is able to take his profit, which, due to the high-risk nature of the investment, may be high.

EXAMPLE

The potential of the BES to help achieve profitable investments in unquoted companies can be illustrated as follows:

It is assumed that the company is carrying on a qualifying trade and that it has been doing so for at least four months (in order that a relief claim can be made). The investor is assumed to have a marginal tax rate of 60%.

	£
Cost of shares subscribed for at the original issue	10,000
Amount of tax saved	6,000
Actual cost of investment	4,000

Assuming that the value of the investment doubles over the five-year period:

		£	£
Sale proceeds			20,000
CGT base cost		10,000	
Indexation allowance RPI @ 21.6%*		2,160	12,160
			7,840

* Assuming a 5% rate of inflation compounded over five years.

	£
Proceeds	20,000
Cost (after tax relief)	4,000
Gross gain	16,000
CGT @ 30% (i.e. 30% of £7,840*)	2,352
Net gain	13,648
% increase on actual cost of investment	341

* Assuming that the investor has already used up his annual 'free' capital gains allowance of £5,900.

This example of the tax relief obtained under the Business Expansion Scheme illustrates the return on investment which can be achieved.

The Business Expansion Scheme is set to run for five years, relief being obtainable in all or any of the tax years 1982/83, 1983/84, 1984/85, 1985/86 and 1986/87. The future of the scheme beyond 1987 is uncertain. A great deal depends on the political climate which prevails. However, it is probable that some similar sort of scheme will be introduced, but quite whether it will be as generous as the BES remains to be seen. In the mean time, the impact which the scheme has made on the OTC has been tremendous and the extent of this impact will grow over the five-year period. Obviously, investors may wish to realise their investment after five years and there will be some difficulty in putting a realistic value on their shares and in establishing a market for them. The OTC market, however, is an obvious candidate to provide trading in these shares and an active market would facilitate the establishment of a price, although, with so many similar securities due on the market at about the same time, market values may well be depressed.

7 Taxation and fiscal incentives

Taxation

When discussing the question of taxation with regard to the OTC market two aspects must be considered. From the point of view of the company to be floated, it is essential that a good deal of tax planning is effected at an early stage, so that at the time of flotation the tax consequences for the major shareholders are minimised. In addition, the tax position of the individual investor who is putting money into OTC stocks must be examined.

In preparing for a flotation it is essential that all companies pay attention to tax planning, since it has an important bearing on the whole issue. All routine taxation matters must obviously be covered in detail. The company must be able to show either that any potential liabilities, whether PAYE, VAT or corporation tax, have been settled or at least that the extent of the company's liability has been agreed with the Inland Revenue. Also, from a management point of view, it is essential that it has operated PAYE and

VAT systems effectively. Obviously, a large impending tax liability would be likely to put any public issue of shares in jeopardy.

Prior to flotation it is almost inevitably necessary to undertake considerable restructuring of the company. For example, it is usually necessary to alter the share structure to ensure that there are sufficient shares to issue to the public. Also, where there are certain assets which are not considered to be part of the company to be floated, these are often hived off to the major shareholders or to another company. All such transactions must be cleared with the Inland Revenue before flotation so that any restructuring does not give rise to future tax liabilities. It is essential that the company seeks the advice of professional advisers about these matters. These advisers, which any sponsor will insist that the company appoint, will help the management plan such moves well in advance so that they are achieved with the minimum adverse effect on the company.

From the point of view of the proprietors of the company, mitigation of tax liabilities is again an important issue, and one which must be tackled at an early stage. The flotation of a company often results in a significant increase in the value of a company's shares. This is because a flotation often precedes a period of expansion, as an injection of equity capital from external shareholders provides additional working capital. Certainly, any tax benefits are likely to be greater if changes in shareholdings are effected before the decision to float is taken. In particular, the major shareholders should consider whether they wish to make gifts of shares. Such gifts can be made prior to a flotation without any immediate capital gains tax consequences and may have possible advantages in terms of capital transfer tax because the value that would be attributed to the shares by the Inland Revenue would be appreciably less than the final quoted price. Indeed, careful consideration should be given to the way in which shareholdings are held in any family company. The most important points to consider are the effects of the shareholding in relation to the control of the company and to the shareholders' and the company's tax liabilities. For these reasons the company might consider setting up an Inland Revenue approved share option scheme or establishing a discretionary trust, managed independently, and if necessary an offshore trust fund could be set up. Again, this is a matter that should always be referred to professional advisers.

Taxation considerations are also of prime importance to individual investors. The Business Expansion Scheme is, of course, a major motivating force for private investors in *all* tax brackets. Indeed, it is probably the most effective and straightforward tax shelter currently available under UK tax laws and has already been dealt with in detail in Chapter 6. However, it is worth pointing out again that, while a subscription for new shares in an OTC company may qualify for tax relief under the BES, a subscription for shares in a USM company or in a company which has a full listing on The Stock Exchange will not. This is because, for the purposes of the 1982 Finance Act, shares in OTC companies are considered to be unquoted, even though a market is made in the shares by a licensed dealer.

The fact that the Inland Revenue considers the OTC shares to be 'unquoted' also means that an individual subscriber may claim income tax relief on a loss arising on the disposal of a holding. Furthermore, it is important to note that a share quoted on the OTC is not necessarily valued for tax purposes in the same way as a fully listed share. Because some shares in the OTC market are traded very thinly and, indeed, some of the quotations are 'basis only' (i.e. only an indication), the Inland Revenue will look further than just at the publicly quoted price. They will, in fact, look closely at bargains done on or near the relevant date and may also consider any other influences which could have affected the share prices.

It is the case with most OTC quoted companies that for at least the first trading year on the market dividends are not paid on the shares. As the companies that come to the market-place are usually small and youthful, concern about growth potential can be great. For this reason, capital gain is a primary motive for investment in an OTC company which has only recently been floated and taxpayers in the higher tax brackets will find such investments particularly attractive. This is because additional income in the form of dividends is hit hard by the taxman and capital gains tax is, at present, the lowest tax rate in the United Kingdom. Additionally, each individual has a substantial capital gains tax allowance, which at present means that up to £5,900 of capital gains can be made by any individual in each fiscal year.

Fiscal incentives

As described in Chapter 6, the Business Expansion Scheme has played a major role in providing finance for small and growing businesses. However, with this type of company and start-up situations recognised as the only areas likely to provide substantial employment in real terms in the near future, it has been suggested that further fiscal incentives ought to be introduced to promote this particular sector. Certainly, cutting transaction costs might encourage more people to deal in shares on a regular basis, and in terms of promoting wider share ownership this must be seen as a worthwhile and necessary exercise. However, this would not help the small-company sector specifically, unless, of course, only transactions in small-company equities were exempted from both the transfer stamp and the contract stamp.

A bolder and more radical move would be to exempt individuals and corporations from capital gains tax when dealing in small-company equity instruments. The Chancellor has exempted all gilts' transactions from CGT from July 1986 and the Treasury should now try to promote equity investment in the small company sector. Obviously, this would improve the status of small companies and would encourage investors seriously to consider making investments in this sector, which would directly promote growth and employment. The incentive of capital gains tax exemption is dependent on the merits of any company as an investment and also relates directly to the goal of increasing the share price. Capital gain is the major motivating factor behind the investment decision for many OTC investors, since at present few OTC companies actually pay a dividend. Thus, at a stroke legislators could provide a tremendous boost for investment in the lower market segment. This, in turn, would encourage entrepreneurship and provide an enormous and welcome boost for employment in the United Kingdom. A further consequence would be that entrepreneurs running small- to medium-sized companies would be more willing to part with equity in their company if they knew that they would not be charged capital gains tax. Thus, with the prospects of improved marketability of the shares and tax exemption from the sale of any of his personal shares, the entrepreneur will be encouraged to expand and grow.

An existing fiscal incentive for investors, which as yet has been little used (probably due to the confusion surrounding the subject), is dealt with under section 37 of the 1980 Finance Act. It would appear that losses sustained on trading in both USM and OTC stocks can be set against an individual's income tax bill, provided that the issuing house acted simply as an underwriter and that the shares were in a trading company. At present, however, this particular piece of legislation remains unclear and, although the spirit of the law is favourable, in practice there would seem to be a number of problems in obtaining the relief.

What is clearly needed is a consistent and definitive policy on providing fiscal incentives for small-company equity instruments. This should be widely implemented and publicised in order to stimulate economic growth where it is most needed.

8 The OTC market in the United States

It has been claimed that one of the functions of the OTC market in the United States was to finance the American War of Independence. However, this is mere conjecture, since exact records of where and when the market actually started are scarce, although a reference to transactions in the post-civil war period was made in *Men and Mysteries of Wall Street* by James K. Melbury, dated 1871. In this account one can also see the origins of the term 'over-the-counter'; investors of that period were accustomed to making their purchases and sales of investment securities through private banking houses which, in some of their regular activities as dealers, engaged in the business of buying and selling US government, municipal and corporate bonds. The interior of such banks was not unlike that of the commercial banks of today — there were counters, over which investors directly bought and sold securities. Hence, transactions became known as 'over-the-counter' deals to distinguish them from those effected on the stock markets. In fact, present-day dealers maintain the market as separate from the exchanges and still transact all deals in their offices and so have retained the name 'over-the-counter'.

The OTC market in the United States is far better organised and conducted on a greater scale than in the United Kingdom. It is interesting to consider the US market, as it must surely give an indication of the way the UK market will develop. It is widely believed that as the size and complexity of the OTC in the United Kingdom increases, it will become necessary to introduce the sophisticated electronic price information that is at the very core of the US market.

Development of the US market

During the last 50 years the OTC has grown steadily in the United States, administered by the National Association of Securities Dealers Inc. (NASD). In 1971 a nationwide electronic computer system, NASDAQ (an acronym for National Association of Securities Dealers Automated Quotations), was established to provide a vital communication link between investors, market makers and brokers and brought the OTC market its first real exposure to the public. The system started with quotation information only but has been subsequently expanded to give investors information which was not previously available, such as a running index of stock performance and volume. To give some idea of the impact that computerisation has had upon the market it is worth considering some statistics concerning the NASDAQ market. In its first full year of operation, statistics gathered by NASDAQ's computers showed that some 2.2 billion shares had been traded, confounding critics and sceptics alike. It is the fastest-growing securities market in the world today and ranks first in terms of the number of companies traded in a single market, although the New York Stock Exchange (NYSE) still leads in a number of statistical categories and NASDAQ's trading volume is still only three-quarters that of the NYSE, even though on a daily basis NASDAQ volume has exceeded NYSE volume on a number of occasions. In August 1984 the daily share volume reached an all-time record of 122.2 million shares. Furthermore, NASDAQ volume is nearly three times the combined volume of the remaining major national securities exchanges – the American, Boston, Cincinnati, Midwest, Pacific and Philadelphia Stock Exchanges. In terms of dollar volume of equity trading, NASDAQ turned over some $188.3 billion worth of stock in 1983 and $153.5 billion in 1984. This puts NASDAQ as the third largest market in the world, behind Tokyo ($235.1 billion in 1983 and $267.5 billion in 1984) and the NYSE ($765.3 billion in 1983 and $764.7 billion in 1984).

The NASDAQ figure far exceeds the amount of trade carried on in other major international exchanges during 1984, for example London ($49 billion), Zurich ($37 billion), West Germany ($29.7 billion) and Paris ($12.4 billion). In 1983 there were some 10 million investors who owned OTC securities. While the number of companies listed on the NYSE has dropped slightly over the past five years, the NASDAQ head count has actually risen to a record high of 4,097 companies.

Private investor and company interest

Although the OTC market has been in existence for well over a century in the United States, its early growth has not been well documented, in terms of either development or value. Certainly, early transactions were carried out on a small scale, being completed mainly through the large private banks and financial houses of New York and Boston. In this respect they were fairly insular and were basically private dealings in fully listed stocks. The OTC market, therefore, developed initially as a place to trade listed stocks privately, especially if there was little interest in the stock on the exchanges or if only a very thin market existed in it.

The boom in railroad building called forth huge amounts of external finance for the development of a nationwide rail network. Thus, the OTC became not only a trading market but also a place where money could be raised. Indeed, the inter-war period of economic expansion in the United States saw railroads, public utilities, industrial companies and other corporations use the OTC to obtain long-term finance through a primary distribution of securities. The market continued to grow, particularly as US government bonds began to be traded OTC and as it became the major market for municipal issues (i.e. obligations issued by states and cities). In fact, very few municipal issues were actually listed, with one exception – those of the City of New York municipal bonds, which were traded on the NYSE.

It should be noted that, from a very early stage in the development of the OTC market in the United States, participants were subject both to SEC (Securities Exchange Commission) rules and regulations and to those of the self-regulatory association NASD (see page 92).

The market continued to expand and develop both as a market-place for buying and selling outstanding issues of bonds and stocks and for the sale and distribution of new issues of securities. Indeed, by as early as the 1940s, the OTC market had established itself as the major market in the United States for the initial placing of the securities of investors of new corporations and of municipal and foreign security issues.

In the early stages of the development of the market it is unclear which type of company actively sought and successfully obtained finance through the OTC. Obviously, corporate treasurers had to choose between a full listing on one of the stock exchanges and an OTC quote, where a number of dealers would place the initial stock and continue to make a market in it. Since it is impossible to obtain statistical data from the early part of this century concerning the relative costs of a flotation on the OTC as opposed to a full listing one cannot make any firm conclusion as to why corporations chose to go OTC. However, in an article in the *Wall Street Journal* in 1931, entitled 'Over-the-Counter Possibilities', Meyer Willett suggested that there were certain factors surrounding a bond or stock issue which tended to give it a natural eligibility for and adaptability to trading in the OTC market. He stated that an issue would lend itself more readily to trading OTC if it possessed one or more of the following characteristics:

1 Desirability for investment portfolios of institutions, such as banks and insurance companies.
2 Limited distribution.
3 Absence of speculative interest.
4 High price.
5 Small capitalisation.

These criteria may appear strange in the light of recent events on the UK market but are very similar to those applied by Granville & Co., which, as already explained, was responsible for establishing the OTC in the United Kingdom. With an increase in investor interest and in the number of corporations seeking long-term finance, the market expanded rapidly in both size and the number of centres where trading took place.

Although Wall Street remained the major centre for OTC trading, firms of broker-dealers specialising in OTC stocks were established in Chicago, Boston, Philadelphia, Los Angeles, San Francisco, Buffalo, Baltimore, Denver and St Louis. Thus, the influence and scope of the market became widespread and it became established as perhaps the major market-place in the United States for the raising of new capital.

Growth of the US market

However, for all the developments that took place during the nineteenth century, which transformed the market from its humble beginnings in private banking houses in New York into the major mechanism for raising capital, the OTC was still regarded as a secondary market. As a junior market, it was a place where small companies 'grew up' until they were ready for a full exchange listing. In spite of the size of the market, which was by the 1970s turning over hundreds of millions of dollars in shares, it was largely unrecognised, which is the main reason why so little has actually been written about it.

In 1971 the National Association of Securities Dealers (NASD) created the NASDAQ system using modern computer and communications technology. The system transformed the nature of OTC trading, which previously had been rather chaotic. Before NASDAQ came into operation, recent price quotations for OTC securities were elusive. Messengers scrambled to deliver pink sheets, which gave price quotations that were hours or even days old. For a more recent quote a broker had to contact a market maker by telephone or telegraph. Shopping for the best quotation among the various market makers was practicable only for large orders. It was therefore not surprising that promising companies fled the OTC market for the relative calm and organisation of the major exchanges, the climate changing only when NASDAQ began operation as a prototype for the stock exchange of the future. Importantly, NASDAQ gave the OTC market public visibility, which it had largely lacked. Indeed, hitherto many investors had considered the OTC market to be a chaotic backwater of the securities industry.

The impact that NASDAQ has made upon the OTC market in the United States is truly astonishing. Its phenomenal growth in volume must be attributed to the quality of the companies traded in the market and reflects burgeoning investor interest and increased confidence in the NASDAQ system. A total of 10 million shareholders now own OTC securities, virtually double the number in 1975. Moreover, recent statistics show that the number of investors who hold OTC securities is continuing to grow at a much more rapid pace than ownership of exchange listed securities – clear evidence that the market continues to develop and grow. After all, it is still money that moves any market and investor capital is flowing increasingly into NASDAQ companies. The price performance of NASDAQ securities has doubtless provided additional impetus for growing investor interest. For example, the NASDAQ Composite Index has outpaced the Standard and Poor's 500 Index (roughly equivalent to the FT 30 Index in the United Kingdom) as well as most other broadly-based market indices over a period of several years.

In the light of this track record, it is not surprising that many successful NASDAQ companies no longer seek an exchange listing once they become eligible and NASDAQ issues represent a wide spectrum of companies from every sector. The major factor that keeps companies on the OTC is the fact that, regardless of their size, all NASDAQ companies derive broad support for their securities from the competitive market-maker system which characterises the OTC market. Indeed, a clear majority of chief executive officers of NASDAQ quoted companies who participated in a NASD sponsored survey cited multiple market makers as a major advantage over the single-specialist system of the exchanges. It would seem that the existence of several market makers who are all prepared to commit capital (in that they hold lines of stock in those companies in which they make a market) provides the market with greater depth and liquidity. A study under-taken by the Department of Finance at Texas A & M University gave some theoretical credence to this widely held belief. The report, entitled 'Liquidity, Exchange Listing and Common Stock Performance', examined the relationship between common stock liquidity and both exchange listing and price behaviour during major fluctuations in the market. The study concluded that OTC liquidity tends to dominate AMEX (American Stock Exchange) liquidity for stocks of the same size. It was noted that, for most size ranges of companies, NYSE listing may imply a lower liquidity than had the company remained OTC and it was felt that this greater liquidity probably resulted from the interest of multiple market makers in their stocks. The authors went on to say that 'Our study results add to a growing body of evidence that exchange listing is of little (or at least questionable) benefit to companies.' The significance of this statement may well prove relevant to the UK stock markets after the deregulation scheduled for 1986.

Thus, the market has proved to be popular with investors and companies alike and there is evidence to suggest that the market continues to grow apace.

Regulating the US market

The securities business is one of the most highly regulated fields of private enterprise in the United States. It is regulated both by the individual states and by the federal government. State laws vary from one state to the next but are generally well established and recognised by the courts. Federal regulation is achieved principally through the Securities Act of 1933 and the Securities Exchange Act of 1934. The former provides for the full and fair disclosure of information about new securities and new offerings of old securities. Basically, it is concerned with all phases of new financing of business and industry and with the distribution of securities to investors. The latter provides for the regulation of US securities exchanges and transactions on them and also for the regulation of transactions in the OTC market.

Both Acts are administered by the Securities and Exchange Commission (SEC), which was itself set up in 1934 and which is one of several independent, quasi-judicial regulatory agencies of the United States federal government. It has responsibility for most aspects of regulation, covering both the activities of securities firms and the issue of securities by companies. The two Acts under which the SEC derives its authority tend to contain broad statutory policies, delegating to the SEC the power to promulgate and implement the rules and to define relevant terms. The SEC has extensive investigative powers, including the right to subpoena witnesses and documents. Failure to comply with its orders is punishable by fines and imprisonment. It can also apply to the courts for injunctions proscribing behaviour which might constitute violation of the Acts which it administers. Any changes in the rules and regulations of the stock exchanges or of NASD must now, in practice, first be approved by it, and any new issue of securities in the United States has to be registered with it. The SEC has a staff of approximately 2,000 people, a large proportion of whom are lawyers, and is governed by five commissioners, each appointed for fixed five-year terms by the President of the United States, subject to confirmation by the Senate.

The main points of the two Acts, as they affect the OTC market, are as follows:

1 Registration of new security issues must be made with the SEC and the prospectuses used in the sale of such securities must provide full and fair disclosure of information to prospective buyers.
2 Regulation of the sale of securities is achieved primarily by imposing liabilities for the sale of any securities by means of fraud or misrepresentation.

3   All brokers and dealers in the OTC market must be registered with the SEC.
4   The conduct of all dealers is supervised and regulated by the SEC in accordance with the Act.

NASD

In addition to these statutory regulations, administered by the SEC, the OTC market is also supervised by the National Association of Securities Dealers (NASD). The original Securities Exchange Act of 1934 severely limited the role that any self-regulatory body could play. However, the Maloney Act of 1938 amended the Securities Exchange Act and permitted associations of dealers and brokers to be formed. Any such body had to be registered with the SEC and, with its approval, could both make and enforce rules and regulations for its members regarding standards and practices of business carried out in the OTC market. Hence, in 1939 NASD was registered with the SEC as a national, self-regulatory non-profit making body for the OTC market. Today there are some 5,726 broker-dealer firms, including nearly all of the members of stock exchanges doing public business belonging to NASD. Some 330,000 registered representatives of these organisations are subject to NASD regulation. It is fair to say that current-day activities of NASD extend far beyond the straightforward regulations of its members. Working closely with the SEC, NASD sets standards for NASDAQ securities and market makers and provides ongoing surveillance of trading activities. NASD also provides key services for its membership and NASDAQ companies, particularly through its co-operative efforts with governmental and other agencies on policies and legislations which affect the investment, banking and securities business. Indeed, as a regulatory organisation whose activities are geared to protect investors and to promote fair business practices, NASD determines the compliance of brokers and dealers with both governmental regulations and its own Rules of Fair Practice.

The management and administration of the affairs of NASD are the responsibility of a board of governors. This board consists of 21 representatives of the securities industry, eight governors-at-large and a president, and together they determine NASD policy on a national scale. In addition to the board, there are 13 district committees, elected by NASD firms in their respective areas. They supervise NASD programmes in the districts and serve as business conduct committees, which review the reports of NASD examiners, conduct disciplinary proceedings and impose penalties for violations of federal and state laws and of NASD's Rules of Fair Practice.

The NASDAQ system

Before the NASDAQ system came into operation in 1971, the OTC market in the United States had always been a multi-location market made on the telephone, without any central trading floor. But the introduction of this nationwide, highly sophisticated computerised communications system has revolutionised the market-place. The NASDAQ system stores and transmits up-to-the-minute quotations on around 4,700 companies and has a market capitalisation of $206.95 billion. Through the network some 5,700 broker-dealers are linked together, enabling them to know virtually instantaneously the terms currently offered by all the major dealers in securities covered by the system. Furthermore, professional traders and investors connected to NASDAQ have immediate access to all dealers so that they can make markets in any particular stock. Because dealers have constant access to their competitors' quotes through the system, quotations seldom drift far apart. On average, there are more than seven market makers competing with each other to buy and sell NASDAQ securities (although there are obviously more for popular stocks; for example, MCI has 28 competing market makers) and if one dealer's quotes fall temporarily out of step with the market competing dealers will find it profitable to sell to or buy from him until he alters his prices. This inter-dealer trading, coupled with the visibility made possible by NASDAQ, is undoubtedly an important factor in maintaining a closely competitive market, with narrow bid/offer spreads.

The information display system operates at three levels. Broker-dealers which subscribe to level three are given terminals with which to enter bid and firm offer prices for any stock in which they make a market. These market makers must be prepared to execute trades for at least one 'normal unit of trading' (usually 100 shares) at the prices quoted. As soon as a bid or offer price is entered for a security it is placed in a central computer file and may be seen by other subscribers (including other dealers) on their own terminals. Obviously, when new quotations are entered they replace the dealers' former prices.

Most brokerage firms subscribe to level two of the NASDAQ system, obtaining terminals that can display the current quotation on any security in the system. Bid quotations are displayed in descending order and offer quotations in ascending order. The dealer offering each quotation is also identified. Level one of the system is used by individual account executives simply to get an idea of the price of a particular stock. It shows a representative bid and offer price for each security; the former is the median of the current bid prices in the system; the latter is obtained by adding to the representative bid the median bid-offer spread for the stock's current quotation. The system constantly calculates NASDAQ indices, both during and at the end of every trading day. Volume and closing bid and offer prices are then released to the wire services for transmission to newspapers. Another attraction of a NASDAQ listing is that it has lower entry costs. The maximum fee payable by a company to have its stock traded in the system is $5,000. This compares favourably with AMEX ($15,000) and the NYSE ($29,350).

NASDAQ stocks are, in fact, a rather élite group within the OTC in the United States; only one-third of companies traded OTC are part of the electronic market. The reason for this is that there are a number of qualifying standards which must be met for inclusion in the system and continuing, though less stringent, criteria for remaining there, details of which can be seen in Table 2.

Table 2 Qualifying standards for NASDAQ and NMS inclusion

Standard	For initial NASDAQ inclusion (domestic common stocks)	For continued NASDAQ inclusion (domestic common stocks)	For newspaper national list inclusion		SEC criteria for mandatory NMS inclusion	SEC criteria for voluntary NMS inclusion
			Alternative 1	Alternative 2		
Registration under section 12(g) of the Securities Exchange Act of 1934 or equivalent	Yes	Yes	Yes	Yes	Yes	Yes
Total assets	$2 million	$750,000	$2 million	$2 million	–	–
Tangible assets	–	–	–	–	$2 million	$2 million
Capital and surplus	$1 million	$375,000	$1 million	$8 million	$1 million	$1 million
Net income	–	–	$300,000 in latest or 2 of 3 last fiscal years	–	–	–
Operating history	–	–	–	4 years	–	–
Public float (shares)	100,000	100,000	350,000	800,000	500,000	250,000
Market value of float	–	–	$2 million	$8 million	$5 million	$3 million
Minimum bid	–	–	$3	–	$10 on 5 business days	$5 on 5 business days
Trading volume	–	–	–	–	Average 600,000 shares/month for 6 months	Average 100,000 shares/month for 6 months
Shareholders of record	300	300	300	300	300	300
Number of market makers	2	1	2	2	4 on 5 business days	4 on 5 business days

Source: NASDAQ Fact Book 1983, produced by the National Association of Securities Dealers Inc.

Shares must be registered under section 12(g) of the Securities Exchange Act 1934, which creates the need for the onerous reporting requirements characteristic of US stock markets. However, what has made the NASDAQ system popular is that NASDAQ require no additional reporting requirements, as is the case for both AMEX and NYSE stocks. For example, the NYSE insists that all common shareholders should have equal voting rights and this has undoubtedly deterred companies from seeking a 'big board' listing.

What has particularly attracted high-growth companies to NASDAQ and contributed to its astonishing growth is the creation of the National Market System (NMS). This was set up on 1 June 1982, the culmination of several years of planning, in response to a 1975 congressional mandate for the use of new technology to link the various markets to create a broader, more efficient competitive national market system. The NMS reports, on terminal screens, all sale, bid and offer prices within 90 seconds of each trade. At the end of the day, total volume and high, low and closing prices are available, rather than only the best closing bid and offer prices which is traditional for NASDAQ stocks.

The NMS was initiated with what the SEC designated as tier 2 companies, i.e. those meeting certain financial and market criteria. These companies must have had an average trading volume of 600,000 shares a month for the past 6 months and have at least 500,000 shares in public hands, a minimum bid price of $10 and a minimum of four market makers. Tier 2 companies are also designated as qualifying for voluntary participation. Details of SEC criteria for mandatory and voluntary NMS inclusion can be seen in Table 2. In December 1984 there were 1,180 securities traded on the NMS, and in November 1984 NASD's proposal to the SEC was accepted and now all 'tier 2' stocks will be included and this will greatly increase the number of NMS stocks to around 2,600. This system, together with the myriad of market makers available in the OTC system, offers a trading exposure that appeals to many new companies.

In addition, NMS qualifying companies now enjoy perks that only an exchange listing used to confer, such as daily, nationwide newspaper visibility. The average company traded on the NMS is of some substance; the average share price is $15.14, with average assets of $572.7 million and a revenue of around $181.2 million. In addition, each company has an average of 11.5 market makers.

One of the most important aspects of NASDAQ is the computerised surveillance system, which helps to police the market and eliminate malpractice. The Market Information Data Access System (MIDAS) puts volume and price parameters around every NASDAQ security. When unusual activity occurs a parameter break is set off and market surveillance analysts immediately investigate to determine whether the behaviour of the stock was due to legitimate market forces or to illegal trading practices. This built-in system can provide investigations with historical quotation data on a minute-by-minute basis, allowing the reconstruction of past trading patterns. This facility therefore allows NASDAQ to engage in a full audit into the quotation activities of any market maker should there be any suspicion of improper practices. Market surveillance conducted by NASDAQ also extends to insider dealing abuse, with all investigations of substance being referred to the SEC by NASD.

This high degree of surveillance and monitoring of the market, combined with the high profile of the investigators themselves, has meant increased investor confidence and obvious growing popularity. Furthermore, major institutions have been reassured by this high level of visibility and have increased their involvement in the market accordingly. A key ingredient in the success of the NASDAQ market has been the continued dependability and reliability of the system. An indication of the load placed on it is given by the fact that on average, during 1984 there were over 1.2 million quote requests daily. In addition, there were 16,000 transaction reports and 280,000 quote updates. Despite the increasingly heavy demands placed on the system (1984 saw an increase of 19% to some 122,403 level one terminals in operation) the average response time to a request was around three seconds.

However, with the likelihood of the inclusion of tier 2 companies in the NMS and more companies coming on to the NASDAQ system, even greater demands are likely to be placed on the system. Already, a third computer has been installed at the NASDAQ data centre and NASD has introduced a number of enhancements to the system to keep it at the forefront of electronic share dealing. The Trade Acceptance and Reconciliation Service was introduced in 1983 and was designed as a major advance in resolving trades between firms which fail to compare during clearance and settlement. The expansion of the service will speed up the processing of uncompared trades throughout the OTC market. In 1984 the Small Order Execution System was introduced and, although operating on a relatively small scale at first, this will equip market makers with the capability to handle greater volume more efficiently. The system automatically executes small orders against the best quotations. Furthermore, the whole NASDAQ system is due to be upgraded from its present 125 million shares a day capacity to 200 million shares a day. Thus, the system is being constantly improved and NASD, in the face of competition from the main exchanges, is striving to take full advantage of the system's potential by introducing new products, such as options trading.

NASDAQ versus conventional exchanges

The whole NASDAQ system, now in its second decade, has established itself as a major international market. Approximately 215 foreign securities and 81 American Depository Receipts (ADRs) are listed on the system, with a dollar volume trading in excess of £75 billion. The UK companies with ADR representation include, among others, Glaxo,

British Telecom, Fisons and Beechams. Hard Rock Cafe and Harvard Securities Group PLC, quoted on the OTC in the United Kingdom, are also listed in ADR form on NASDAQ.

It must be noted that this challenge to the conventional stock markets has grown within the auspices of the SEC but has not been totally unopposed. Increasingly, NASDAQ has attracted high-profile companies to the detriment of the NYSE and what is significant is that these companies are staying on the system. In fact, some 600 OTC companies now qualify for the 'big board' exchanges but have chosen to remain on the OTC. Included in this figure are a number of very large, well-known companies, such as Intel, MCI and Apple Computers, who prefer the OTC market because they would rather have competitive market makers than a single exchange specialist. The market makers frequently commit combined capital that far exceeds the resources of the exchange specialist who maintains the market for a similar listed security. This competition has led to widespread debate on the relative merits of the two systems, which will become increasingly relevant to the UK stock markets.

On one side of the argument are those who believe in the auction system as practised on AMEX and the NYSE. On the NYSE, for instance, there are currently 412 specialists, grouped into 56 firms, who control trading in one or more stocks. Specialists in this situation are required to risk their own capital if necessary in order to maintain fair and orderly markets. Mr John J. Phelan, chairman and chief executive officer of the NYSE, claims that the exchange remains the most efficient system for protecting the public against trading-related abuses. On the other hand, supporters of the NASDAQ system believe that it provides for a much less volatile market and results in fairer pricing of securities. This argument has recently received considerable support – Mr William McGowan, chairman of MCI, the

largest stock traded OTC in the United States, criticised the
NYSE's specialist dealer system and compared it unfavour-
ably to the NASDAQ approach of allowing competing
market makers. Similarly, Mr S. DeVaughn, a spokesman
for Apple Computers, in defending the company's decision
to remain on the OTC market, called an exchange listing
'expensive' and maintained that 'you are at the mercy of a
specialist'. Block trading business is an important activity
on the NYSE. There, a broker-dealer which seeks large
numbers of matching orders for an institution is prepared to
quote a firm price to the originating client and, if necessary,
to position against all or part of the order if it is not able to
find matching orders.

Regional exchanges have established niches for themselves and they do provide some competition for AMEX
and the NYSE. However, it is the specialist trading system
which lies at the heart of the main exchanges and critics
maintain that this has failed to evolve in step with changes
in the securities industry and, as a result, they have become
far less attractive to individual companies. In fact, the
number of listings on the NYSE has dropped by about
one-third over the past ten years. Certainly, the NYSE
seems to be taking the challenge of NASDAQ seriously. It is
believed to be considering a move to 24-hour trading and,
indeed, in a world where 24-hour, global securities trading
is becoming a reality, the big board's adherence to its
specialist system geared on bankers' hours seems rooted in
the past. AMEX, too, is considering the possibility of
extending its trading hours. NASDAQ is currently open for
trading nine hours a day, while the NYSE operates between
10 a.m. and 4 p.m. only. A number of new products are also
being considered by the main exchanges, such as trading in
futures, and in March 1984 the NYSE was granted by the
SEC the right to begin trading on two options of indexes
made up of a handful of stocks.

The NYSE has also decided to make it easier for big

brokerage houses to buy into specialist market makers, which carry out most of the trading on the floor. If this move goes through then much-needed capital will be injected into these specialist firms. Furthermore, the NYSE is reviewing its entry requirements, making it easier for companies to obtain a listing and more difficult for them to be thrown off the exchange. The big board exchanges are also under pressure to strengthen their ties with the rapidly diversifying brokerage firms, which see market making in certain stocks as a rapidly declining source of revenue.

Even if these changes take place and further new products are introduced and developed, NASDAQ's network of linked computer terminals still poses a threat to the main exchanges, and a more serious one at that, since it does actually represent the future. It is widely believed in the United States that NASDAQ is the way that all stock markets will develop and that the specialist exchange system is already outdated. Quite apart from this, it is interesting to note that the pillars of the US financial world have been forced to sit up and take notice of the OTC market. More importantly, the exchanges have been forced to cast a critical eye over the services they offer and, as a result, are taking steps to become both more competitive and more innovative.

9 The future

Changes to The Stock Exchange

At the time of going to press, the exact form of the proposed changes to the structure of The Stock Exchange is not known. However, it is generally accepted that the minimum scale of commission will be abolished, which will put pressure on brokers to trade between themselves and, in so doing, to cut out the jobber. The result of this will probably be the emergence of a dual- rather than a single-capacity system, with firms of broker-dealers able to trade either as agents or as principals.

This threat to the single-capacity system (in which the functions of broker and jobber are carried out by two different people) has caused much consternation in the City. Many people believe that the single-capacity system offers the best protection to investors, although it is clear that when it was first introduced at the turn of the century investor protection was not a major issue. In fact, moves by the Stock Exchange Committee in 1908 to unify brokers and jobbers were brought about as a direct result of the need for them to be protected from each other rather than for the public to be protected. These moves forbade brokers from acting as dealers and making prices, and jobbers from dealing direct with non-Stock Exchange members rather than through brokers. In 1911 The Stock Exchange also introduced a scale of fixed commissions, which prevented jobbers from using so-called 'dummy brokers' – brokers employed by a jobber at a nominal cost to pass a bargain through.

With the proposed termination of the distinction between stockbrokers and stockjobbers (the single-capacity system), it is widely believed that the traditional trading floor will be replaced by its electronic equivalent. Dealings will be carried out via a central computer with broker-dealers working from their own offices.

How these changes will affect the OTC

These changes in the structure of The Stock Exchange, designed primarily to make UK securities markets more competitive in an increasingly international environment, will mean that knock-on effects will be felt in other markets. Indeed, these radical reforms, due to be introduced by the end of 1986, will have far-reaching consequences for the OTC market. The new centralised dealing system, resulting from the new dual-capacity system, with market makers quoting competing prices in selected stocks, will be very similar to current practice in the OTC. This means that members of the public will have to contact a number of broker-dealers to find out which is quoting the best prices in, for example, ICI or Glaxo. Obviously, competition among the broker-dealers for business will mean that the prices quoted are the best possible at that particular moment. This is exactly what happens at present on the OTC market, except that when this system is introduced on the London Stock Exchange there will be a far larger number of market makers in popular stocks than exist at the moment in OTC stocks. A comparable example may be the NASDAQ system in the OTC in the United States, where popular issues may have more than 20 competing market makers.

There has been a certain degree of uneasiness concerning the dual-capacity function of licensed dealers, however. Doubts have been expressed concerning the integrity of dealings carried out by a firm which is acting as both principal and agent. Sceptics find it hard to believe that these two functions of a dealer can be kept completely separate, and that no conflict of interest, if arising at all, can be tolerated. However, once the major markets adopt a similar method of dealing and dual capacity becomes accepted as common practice (as it has always been in the United States), it is likely that criticism of the OTC will subside and that its activities will become much more acceptable to the financial community.

With the advent of broker-dealers, whereby brokers and jobbers will be able to merge and become competing market makers, the jobber is certain to lose his monopoly position. Already a number of the larger firms of jobbers are making it clear that they will not feel duty-bound to make a book in unfashionable and consequently unprofitable issues. All the major firms will want to compete for the business in, for example, GEC and Marks & Spencer, but who will make a market in small, fully listed companies that few have ever heard of? It has been suggested that an electronic system of matched orders for the least active issues, in which no market makers were prepared to deal on a regular basis, could be installed. However, it seems unlikely that such a sophisticated system could be put into operation very quickly. Moreover, consideration would also have to be given to the question of who foots the bill for such an expensive system, especially when it would be concerned with relatively inactive issues.

It seems, therefore, that the smaller public company must be wary of the future marketability of its shares. The top 100 equities account for around 60% of total Stock Exchange business, leaving around 7,000 other securities to make up the balance. Even if an electronic 'matching' system could be introduced at a reasonable cost and before minimum commissions are abolished, the investor would be provided with a system that merely paired off buyers and sellers. Thus, if anyone wished to sell a holding in a small, less fashionable company it is likely that he would have to leave his order on the system for matching if and when a buyer emerged. In a bear market, it would be impossible to sell shares in this way and the overall degree of liquidity involved in any such system would not be to the advantage of the investor.

One method for the listed, 'out of the way' company to obtain better liquidity and a continuous two-way market for its shares would be to come to the OTC market. Market makers would be prepared to make a book in these smaller issues, creating far better liquidity both for existing shareholders and for potential investors. It seems likely that many holders of second- and third-line stocks currently listed on The Stock Exchange will see the advantages of an OTC quote and have their listing transferred. If this were to happen, it would mean a marked increase in the size of the OTC market in a very short space of time. Literally hundreds of companies could come to the OTC seeking a listing and, although licensed dealers would need to strengthen their working capital, since they would be running a larger book, this would be a major boost for the OTC market.

A further consequence of permitting broker-dealers to set up in business, combining the roles of jobber and agent, is that The Stock Exchange will become even more concentrated. Only the big firms will have the financial muscle to compete in the major mainline stocks as broker-dealers.

Brokers who wish to retain their single-capacity status may find survival difficult. Institutions are almost certain to deal direct with the market maker, cutting out the middleman and also much of the expense. In addition, the small private client may well be ignored as power is concentrated in fewer and fewer hands. Licensed dealers, therefore, whose market niche covers small companies and private clients, look set to do well out of the proposed reforms.

One particular development which will emerge from all the changes that are to take place will be the widespread review of regulations which it will be necessary to undertake. Indeed, in view of the proposed dual-capacity system, a new, widespread regulatory framework will have to be implemented. Whatever form this takes, it should be understood that strong investor protection measures will be to the benefit not only of investors themselves, but also of the securities industry as a whole.

Although dual capacity seems to have been quite widely accepted by the broking/jobbing community, the issue of whether or not a central trading floor will remain has been far more contentious. Although, logically, a centralised market-place will become redundant when there is a computerised communications system in existence which is sufficiently sophisticated to relay all the necessary information, traditionalists still feel that 'the floor' is essential. Initially, while the transition is being made, a central trading floor may be retained but, in the long term, such an anachronistic feature must disappear and the OTC model for dealing in stocks and shares over the telephone (albeit based on the US experience) will become the standard way of buying or selling securities. The investing public of the United Kingdom will, as a result, become more adept at and attuned to dealing directly with a market maker on the telephone and being quoted a two-way price for dealing. This will also reduce criticism about the way that dealings on the OTC market are conducted directly over the telephone and, once again, mean that the market as a whole will gain in credence.

Developments in the UK market

All future developments in the market are so subject to external factors that any attempt to predict an accurate critical path which the OTC market will follow would be of little value. The attitudes of the Government, the permanent civil servants who staff the higher echelons of the Department of Trade and Industry, The Stock Exchange and, for that matter, all other participants in the financial services field will have an important bearing on the future of the OTC market.

With so many interested parties, a number of them trying to protect vested interests, a consensus on the OTC would be hard to obtain. However, it is expected that the OTC will dramatically increase in size, at the same time becoming increasingly recognised as a legitimate part of the financing structure of the United Kingdom. This in turn will increase the profile of the market. However, if the market is to continue to grow at its current rate a large influx of capital will be needed. Indeed, it is likely that greater institutional involvement will become necessary as more and more companies which gain an OTC listing are financed out of the market's capital base. Although it is not certain whether or not financing institutions will choose to involve themselves in some capacity with the OTC, Citibank has, in a sense, given some indication of how it sees itself developing in the increasingly liberalised UK market in that it has recently completed one USM issue and has three or four in the pipeline. This will be the first time that a foreign bank has sponsored an issue of shares on the London market, but Citibank clearly has the intention of becoming a major corporate finance house. It already has a venture capital group and when Stock Exchange rules permit it will own the merged businesses of Scrimgeour, Vickers da Costa and Kemp-Gee.

This move into the corporate financing of unlisted companies may, indeed, herald a further expansion into the OTC market. Financiers in the United States, including the major banks, should be able to recognise more than anyone the vast potential that the UK market currently holds. They have experienced at first hand the explosive growth of the American OTC and, since the UK market is developing in a very similar fashion (albeit ten years behind), the Americans, acknowledged for being financial innovators, may well wish to participate in the future development of the OTC in the United Kingdom. Whether this participation will take the form of direct involvement, with, for example, US financiers either setting up a dealership in competition with existing firms or injecting capital into the market by taking a stake in one of them, remains to be seen. However, the financial community in the United Kingdom should be aware of the fact that if it is slow to recognise the potential of the OTC it is possible, and even likely, that the United States will become involved in the UK market.

Apart from the introduction of more capital to the market and the involvement of more people in the market (the present number of 15 active market-making firms is far too small to make for a truly liquid market), another major development that may well take place is the recognition of the OTC as a legitimate market. The Stock Exchange has never been enamoured with the idea of an OTC market, primarily because it represented a competitor over which it had no control. However, with the current realignment taking place in the structure of The Stock Exchange, an opportunity has presented itself to its council to endorse the market. This is not to say that the market would ever become a part of The Stock Exchange or even reside under its wing. The OTC is never likely to become part of the Establishment, and, indeed, it should never attempt to do so. Its function is to compete, not to co-operate. However, if The Stock Exchange recognised the three-tier market system, this would be to the benefit of all concerned.

At the moment, the distinction between the three segments is very blurred. Double standards are applied because of the lack of clarity concerning the relative market segments and confusion arises due to the fact that the middle tier, although quoted on The Stock Exchange, is termed as unlisted. It is likely that an equity market-place divided up into three clear and differentiated segments would help to avoid any confusion on the part of the private investor and would also help companies seeking finance, since each tier would be seen roughly in terms of level of risk and size of company. The private client could invest in any one segment according to his risk preference, or he could spread his portfolio across all three markets to provide diversification of risk. Similarly, the directors of a company seeking equity finance would be able to identify quickly and easily the appropriate market-place, the main criteria being the company's stage of maturity. Moreover, there is no doubt that a definite, agreed structure, which was fully supported and recognised by all major participants, would greatly benefit the securities industry of the United Kingdom.

A European OTC

In recent years there have been widespread efforts both to create and to restructure market segments in the European Community. It seems that the idea, prevalent in the 1960s and 1970s, that all stock exchanges must be organised on a standard model appears to have faded. This model was based on uniformly high disclosure requirements and a homogeneous trading system and led to a highly safeguarded and regulated market. It was not only in the United Kingdom that this idea was respected – indeed, most stock markets world-wide seemed to neglect the need for secondary markets specialising in small companies. However, the groundswell of opinion throughout the European community that traditional and ailing industries should be rejuvenated to create much-needed employment has forced financial regulators to think again about the structure of financial markets. Perhaps the most well known of the 'junior' stock markets which now exist are the Unlisted Securities Markets in the United Kingdom and in Ireland, the *Deuxième Marche* in France, the *Parellelmarket* in Amsterdam and the Share Market III in Denmark. These are all secondary market-places but even more recently there has been a widespread acceptance of third-tier markets. Obviously, the OTC market in the United Kingdom has been an important development in the vertical segmentation of the UK securities markets. In Germany, the *Ungeregelter Freiverkehr* has been rediscovered as a tier specialising in small, young unlisted companies and Belgium is also planning to reorganise the daily auctions of unlisted securities in order to gear the market more closely to the needs of smaller companies. Greece, too, is considering a new, semi-official market for small-company shares. Obviously, there is no need for every country to have differentiated segments: much is dependent on the size and sophistication of the particular economy that any financial infrastructure must support. One segment alone may well suffice for largely rural, undeveloped countries, but it is clearly desirable in industrialised states for some degree of vertical segmentation to occur.

Despite a number of differences between one country and another, the developments which have brought about the facility for small- and medium-sized companies to gain a market for their equity instruments show a consistent move towards clearly segmented stock markets. In some European countries (including the United Kingdom), however, there is still a need to increase the general acceptance of a bottom-level segment and to encourage its use. Where a country has a need for such a third-tier stock market no stock exchange should be allowed to enjoy a monopoly over the organisation of that country's other markets.

Outside Europe similar developments are taking place with respect to the introduction of second-tier stock markets. In South Africa the Johannesburg Stock Exchange only very recently announced its new Development Capital Market, designed for the smaller, growing company which is not eligible for a full listing. This market, based loosely on the USM model, is hoping to attract high-risk, expanding companies which are eager for capital. Participants in the market feel that it is satisfying a real need and that investment demand will be stimulated due to the fact that it is now possible to become involved at a relatively early stage in the life of comparatively small companies.

Only the beginning

The OTC market in the United Kingdom is here and here to stay. Those who ignore it do so at their peril. This new market satisfies a real demand, creating and stimulating opportunity and employment. The future for this market-place is tremendously exciting and in ten years there will be a fully established market, with 4,000–5,000 companies quoted, some 50–100 market makers and significant institutional interest.

Appendix I: OTC market makers in the United Kingdom

Market maker	Tel.	Prestel/ Reuters
Afcor Investments Ltd (26)	01-387 9111	–
Baynard Securities Ltd (14)	01-236 6224	–
Chartwell Securities (19)	01-377 1333	–
N. K. Cosgrave & Co. Ltd (11)	01-582 2383	–
Fox Milton & Co. Ltd (2)	01-248 2417	–
Peter Gavagan (2)	061-832 8112	–
General & Overseas Trust Ltd (7)	01-286 9477 01-588 2084	–
Harvard Securities Ltd (85)	01-928 8691	*30955#
Prior Harwin Securities Ltd (21)	01-920 0652	–
Procroft Ltd (2)	01-493 3137	–
Ravendale Securities Ltd (6)	01-629 5983	–
Schroder Securities (UK) Ltd (2)	01-623 3322	–
Security Exchange Ltd (1)	01-588 7352	–
Singer & Friedlander Ltd (2)	01-623 3000	–
UTC Securities Management Ltd (19)	01-258 0183	–

Note: Number of issues traded in parentheses.

Appendix II: A typical timetable for an OTC flotation

Month one
1 Prepare a detailed business plan for distribution to potential sponsors.
2 Examine and, if necessary, make new tax arrangements for existing shareholders and consider the potential benefits of a share option scheme.
3 Exploratory talks held between the issuing house and the company to discuss the basis of the flotation.
4 Formal offer made.

Month two
1 Professional advisers appointed by the sponsor.
2 Preparatory work on draft long-form report started by the reporting accountant.
3 Detailed timetable of events laid down.
4 First rough draft of prospectus produced.

Month three
1 Discuss draft long-form reports produced by the reporting accountants.

2   Regular meetings to redraft the prospectus and to check on the progress of the issue.
3   Profit and cash-flow forecasts finalised by the accountants.
4   Drafts of all issue documentation prepared and circulated.
5   Share price and number of shares to be floated finalised.
6   Directors' service agreements arranged.
7   Accountants confirm indebtedness.

Month four
1   Final proof of prospectus produced/final proof of Extel card.
2   Board meeting to review the prospectus and complete the verification of the prospectus contents.
3   Sign and deliver the documents to the Registrar of Companies.
4   Print the prospectus.
5   Place 'tombstone' advertisements.
6   Press conference held.
7   Subscription lists open/cheques received/allotment letters posted.
8   Dealings in shares start.

Index